Should

World Population?

Political Theory Today

Janna Thompson, *Should Current Generations Make Reparation for Slavery?*
Christopher Bertram, *Do States Have the Right to Exclude Immigrants?*
Diana Coole, *Should We Control World Population?*

Diana Coole

Should We Control World Population?

polity

First published in 2018 by Polity Press

Polity Press
65 Bridge Street
Cambridge CB2 1UR, UK

Polity Press
101 Station Landing
Suite 300
Medford, MA 02155, USA

ISBN-13: 978-1-5095-2340-5
ISBN-13: 978-1-5095-2341-2(pb)

A catalogue record for this book is available from the British Library.

Library of Congress Cataloging-in-Publication Data

Names: Coole, Diana H., author.
Title: Should we control world population? / Diana Coole.
Description: Medford, MA : Polity Press, [2018] | Series: Political theory today | Includes bibliographical references and index.
Identifiers: LCCN 2018000380 (print) | LCCN 2018005762 (ebook) | ISBN 9781509523443 (Epub) | ISBN 9781509523405 (hardback) | ISBN 9781509523412 (pbk.)
Subjects: LCSH: Population policy--Moral and ethical aspects. | Reproductive rights. | Birth control. | Overpopulation.
Classification: LCC HB883.5 (ebook) | LCC HB883.5 .C66 2018 (print) | DDC 363.9--dc23
LC record available at https://lccn.loc.gov/2018000380

Typeset in 11 on 15 Sabon by Servis Filmsetting Ltd, Stockport, Cheshire
Printed and bound in the United Kingdom by Clays Ltd, Elcograf S.p.A

For further information on Polity, visit our website: politybooks.com

Contents

Introduction

Since 1950, the world's population has trebled, from around 2.5 billion to more than 7.5 billion in 2017. It is projected to exceed 9.7 billion by mid-century, rising to around 11.2 billion by 2100. Given a simultaneous rise in living standards and in environmental degradation, it seems timely to ask whether such numbers are sustainable. Demographic change can have enormous national as well as global impacts, especially if a population is growing (or diminishing) significantly. Higher densities affect everyday lives; more (or fewer) people may place substantial strains on social and ecological services; shifts in the ratio between births and deaths alter a country's age profile and economic prospects. In short, demography matters. But should governments therefore try to control trends that are judged sub-optimal? This became one of the most bitterly contested issues of the twentieth century. Today, the outstanding question is not whether massive increases will continue indefinitely but, rather, whether the pace of fertility decline and slowing growth rates now witnessed virtually everywhere will, if left untended, yield a sustainable population within the constraints of the biosphere. If not, strenuous political efforts may be needed to achieve it. But can they be justified ethically?

Population control is commonly (although not necessarily) identified with reducing, even reversing, population growth. This only emerged as a serious issue during the eighteenth century, especially in 'old' countries like Britain that were already considered 'over-peopled'. Industrialization showed that resources were more elastic than previously imagined. The idea of ending worldwide expansion of human numbers only emerged during the mid-twentieth century, with the appearance of new ecological sensibilities that recognized planet Earth as a single but fragile life-support system on which billions now depended. In 'overdeveloped' nations, evidence of environmental deterioration was attributed to the combination of a post-war baby boom and rising production and consumption; in 'underdeveloped' nations, rapid population growth was understood as an obstacle to development and a catalyst for an impending humanitarian crisis. The 1960s and 1970s were the heyday for heroic population-control narratives and policy initiatives that have since been disavowed as coercive. This is the core concern that any new intervention will need to address.

Despite the topic remaining toxic, there are renewed claims that world population growth is contributing significantly to a planetary environmental crisis and calls for government action to reduce it. The terminology of 'population control' is absent from this contemporary discourse but a goal of 'population stabilization' is not. In fact, most nations do practise interventionist policies: a majority of the 197 countries surveyed by the United Nations (UN) in 2013 reported policies for raising or reducing growth rates, primarily through influencing fertility behaviour. The population question has not been much discussed over recent decades but, as it re-emerges, it seems important to revisit and update arguments, taking into account the unprecedented biophysical circumstances, altered geopolitical relationships and novel discursive resources of the twenty-first century.

Three principal variables determine demographic trajectories: fertility, mortality and migration. Public interventions designed to increase life expectancy are commonplace and seldom questioned, although debates about voluntary euthanasia and the right to die are still in their infancy. Certainly, measures designed to limit numbers by raising the death rate would be universally reviled. Population control is primarily interested in fertility rates. 'Future population growth is highly dependent on the path that future fertility will take, as relatively small changes in fertility behaviour, when projected over several decades, can generate large differences in total population.'[1] Population control is defined in this book as *a policy regime designed to modify fertility trends through deliberate interference in reproductive behaviour, with the aim of influencing demographic outcomes*. The total fertility rate (TFR) is the crucial variable here: in simplified terms, it refers to the average number of children a woman will bear over her lifetime. Over time, replacement-level TFR (of 2.1) results in a stable population as each generation replaces itself. To modify the TFR, population controllers must influence individuals' reproductive behaviour. This is not just a complicated undertaking; it is also profoundly controversial. Liberal values of freedom, autonomy and human rights are entangled here with contested definitions of sexuality, gender roles and identities, family norms and embodiment, as well as with ideological disputes over the role of the state and its powers.

Migration, finally, is a somewhat different demographic phenomenon since it refers to the mobility of existing peoples. Migration can nonetheless affect local fertility and death rates. Some environmentalists and security experts warn that increasing numbers may themselves cause mass migrations or life-threatening conflicts. Because of migration's national impact on other demographic variables, immigration and emigration are widely used as policy levers to address perceived size or age imbalances. Regulating people's movement, especially by enforcing national border controls, is both common and contested, although this is not conventionally understood as population control.

The concept of population control contains an ambiguity that is reflected in the book's organization: it refers to both ends and means. *Ends* concern demographic outcomes and associated ambitions to manage them, in order to achieve collective benefits (for the planet and its wildlife, for all or some humans, for future generations). This consequentialist approach is discussed in chapter 1. The question of population control as a matter of *means*, on the other hand, is both interwoven with and logically separate from disagreements about goals. Hostility to population control may stem from a belief that government meddling with private reproductive behaviour in pursuit of demographic ends is inherently coercive and thus illegitimate, irrespective of the merits of the ends pursued. This ethical objection is examined in chapter 2. For other critics, the issue is more practical: regardless of any benefits population policies might bestow on the commons, they doubt there are fair, non-coercive means for pursuing them. This policy dimension is considered in chapter 3.

The book's title is intentionally provocative. By asking 'Should we control world population?', it aims to present a highly controversial topic in a bold and unvarnished way, acknowledging that each term within the question – population, control, we – contributes to its controversial reputation. The concept of *population* is a modern construction born – as Michel Foucault explains – of unprecedented population growth triggered by European development from around 1750, of new statistical techniques capable of aggregating bio-demographic data and measuring trends, of novel (biopolitical) micro-powers capable of permeating and reconstructing everyday habits, of modern states that colonize these techniques and use them to discipline behaviour, of classical political economy's interest in maintaining a productive labour force. Whether contemporary public policy should continue to focus on this aggregated, structural level or on a more micro-level of households and personal choice; whether nations can or should still think of their citizens as a population, given their diversity; whether the numerous but often invisible biopolitical interventions that have become normal features of governance are justifiable: these remain lively questions for critical inquiry.

The idea of *control* is no less politically contentious. Controlling the natural forces that yield bio-demographic phenomena, for example through birth control or disease control, seems congruent with a modern desire to dominate nature through science and action, as a precondition for rational government and personal liberty. Biological connotations of pest control, or political associations with authoritarianism, seem more sinister. The two most familiar examples of population control programmes – China's one-child policy (1979–2016) and the compulsory sterilizations undertaken in India, especially during its State of Emergency (1975–7) – are notorious. Whether they can be justified by their demographic outcomes, and whether any state can legitimately interfere with private family decisions even if it renounces coercive means, raises profound political and ethical questions that are not readily resolved.

This normative terrain is further complicated by new models of governing. During the 1980s, objections that population control is an unjustifiable invasion of privacy became entangled with political rejections of top-down, centralized planning regimes. The 'command-and-control' model that was conducive to managing demographic trends, and the bureaucratic welfare programmes that were congenial to providing comprehensive, goal-driven family planning services, have been displaced by models of decentralized governance associated with neoliberal preferences for privatized risks and services. As political conceptions of individual freedom mesh with economic notions of rational personal choice, definitions of coercion and voluntary consent become less clear-cut. On the other hand, whether it is by a liberal model of government that privileges human rights, or by a neoliberal model of governance that privileges market forces over state action, population control has been reframed by a starker opposition between individual freedom (or choice) and (coercive) state control than was formerly the case. This dichotomy is challenged at several points in the following chapters.

The *we*, finally, poses some particularly intractable political difficulties since it concerns the distribution of power and the identity of the agents who would exert control (or comprise their targets). Do governments have the right to tell (some?) people how many children they may bear when the common good is at stake? Conversely, do couples have a responsibility to take into account the effects on other people, future generations and different species of their procreation? If so, do rulers (or experts) have a role in educating or advising them, and does the public also have a part to play in debating population policies?

The 'we' provokes additional geopolitical critiques, given regional disparities in which uneven demographic trends map onto unequal development. If the planet is unsustainably peopled, who is responsible? Who should act? Some critics challenge the idea of a tragedy of the commons shared by all current and future generations of humans (and other species). In particular, they may reject the blanket suggestion that fewer people are needed to avoid environmental collapse or global injustice, especially if this ignores the diverse contributions and responsibilities of different regions. Given the demographic and economic disparities between the global North and South, and their disproportionate contributions to population growth and environmental degradation, they equate the idea of a worldwide population problem with neo-colonial sophistry. Indeed, some critics deny that a problem of overpopulation exists at all, especially inasmuch as this casts blame on the high-fertility nations of the less developed world, and attribute responsibility for environmental unsustainability entirely to overconsumption in wealthy countries.

Yet others are wary of reducing the 'we' to western interests since this both denies agency to poor countries and neglects adverse effects of rapid population growth on their own interests in development. From a demographic perspective, it seems pragmatic to concentrate on helping regions where population growth is most evident, especially if this impedes their aspirations to eliminate poverty. The principal locus of concern has shifted since the late twentieth century from Asia (with its populous nations and now emergent economies) to Africa (where most least developed countries are situated). 'In all plausible scenarios of future trends, Africa will play a central role in shaping the size and distribution of the world's population over the next few decades.'[2] Yet focusing attention on fertility reduction here provokes accusations of racism and eugenics, a charge exemplified by Hardt and Negri's assertion that it is 'difficult to separate most contemporary projects of population control from a kind of racial panic'.[3] The intersection of causality, blame and interests marks one of the most politically combustible arenas in population disputes.

It could plausibly be argued, however, that it is wealthier nations that are most overpopulated since they have exceeded the capacity of their territories to support their biophysical needs and their members individually make disproportionate claims on world resources. Perhaps, then, it is richer peoples who must assume the responsibilities of the 'we' in limiting their own numbers as well as curtailing their consumption. In this case, what are the responsibilities of emergent economies like China and India (whose 2.7 billion people comprise 37 per cent of the 2017 world population), with their millions of new middle-class consumers and degraded environments? Such questions imply that any renewed debate about world population will need to recognize both the diverse material conditions in which overpopulation occurs (which no longer devolve easily into global North versus South) and a shared (but differentiated) contribution to planetary harm. These are extremely challenging issues, but what they indicate is the importance of reassessing assumptions about the 'we', 'us' and 'them' in a world where demographics, geopolitics and environmental indicators are changing yet inseparable.

Rephrasing the main question in the passive voice – should world population be controlled? – apparently avoids the problem of the 'we' by presenting an objective choice: as inhabitants of the global commons, do we not share a collective interest in controlling our aggregate numbers? This is a legitimate question and, as with climate change, it is in principle feasible to imagine building an international consensus supported by a network of transnational organizations that endorse an overarching discourse compatible with universal human rights. Something like the latter indeed exists, in the form of the so-called 'Cairo consensus': the dominant population discourse since 1994, when it emerged from the UN's International Conference on Population and Development (ICPD). The core of the paradigm shift Cairo represented is, however, a rejection of the 'numbers game' and policies associated with it (that is, of neo-Malthusian reproductive policies whose primary rationale is to halt population growth), and their replacement by a reproductive rights framework. For some current demographers and environmentalists, including climate scientists, the aim is to restore an international political commitment to stabilizing world population (without compromising voluntarism or rights) through the development of a new framework for population policies. Supportive data and empirical evidence abound; it is their political and ethical framework that awaits construction.

One thing is clear: any such constructive undertaking must be located in the material and geopolitical context of the twenty-first century, including its new models of governance and demographic trends. Yet it is unlikely to succeed unless it includes a critical reappraisal of previous population disputes and assessments of their current relevance. This latter genealogy is too complicated to explore in detail here, but the key point is that, during the post-war decades, population matters often served as a proxy or vehicle for wider conflicts (Cold War East/West hostilities; left/right ideological struggles; post-colonial animosities between the global North and South; the febrile politics of gender, race and class; the legacy of eugenics programmes). It is because they continue to cast a long shadow that we need to reassess inherited positions, while finding new ways to think about the interfaces between politics and population. This short book tries to do justice to this multifaceted approach. It identifies outstanding political and ethical questions but asks, in particular, whether 'population control' can be morally and empirically justified.

1

Should Population be Controlled?

Given the impact of population change, is it in societies' interests to control it? This chapter concentrates on the broader question of demographic *ends*. Demographic ends, or goals, concern policies that address a population's growth rate, size and density. Economists, demographers and environmentalists are the principal players in this 'numbers game', in which natural resources, economic development/growth and technological capabilities are especially salient elements. Normative judgements about the quality of life (the wider existential purpose served by managing numbers) are important, too, albeit often dismissed on the grounds that they are difficult to measure or quantify.

Because population control is usually associated with ('neo-Malthusian') efforts to limit fertility in order to reduce growth rates, the chapter mainly focuses on consequentialist arguments for anti-natalist initiatives. It is important to bear in mind, however, that even among advocates of population policies there are disagreements about their direction: that is, whether the aim should be fewer or more people, and thus whether national governments should pursue anti- or pro-natalist policies. This partly reflects the context-sensitive nature of changing demographic impacts, which vary as economic and environmental conditions alter. But it also expresses deeper disagreements about sustained versus limited growth, competing models of wealth creation and development, disputes over how best to achieve environmental sustainability and intergenerational justice, and conflicts over anthropocentric versus biocentric ontologies.

Contrary to some popular misconceptions, population control does not mean culling superfluous people. The aim is to reduce current birth rates in order that smaller future generations might live better. This was essentially Malthus's point in his *Essay on the Principle of Population* (1798): that elective ('preventive') checks on fertility are needed to avoid natural ('positive') checks later since overpopulation raises mortality rates (especially through famine). The temporal structure of such arguments is important but complicated. If the outcome of unregulated population expansion, and thus the longer-term cost of inaction, looks catastrophic, can the benefits of lower numbers justify even coercive means? Later, I will challenge this either/or formula as too simplistic. But my point here is that this classic political dilemma of means versus ends is exacerbated in the case of population growth by difficulties in establishing the severity, imminence and likelihood of future risks. Should the precautionary principle hold? Modelling data-rich scenarios is helpful but it can only inform, not resolve, such normative issues.

Any presumption that it is only, but always, anti-natalist policies that are coercive is also misplaced. It elides two facts: that on the one hand, many successful fertility-reduction programmes have been voluntary (in Thailand and Iran, for example) while also benefiting women; and that on the other, coercive pro-natalist policies which associate large and growing populations with advantageous economic, military or nationalist outcomes have also been prevalent. Romania, where large families effectively became state policy under Ceausescu's regime during the 1980s, is one such example; French policy during the 1940s is another. Identifying coercive pro-natalist policies does not of course justify anti-natalist coercion, but it does correct a bias against population stabilization while underlining the importance of proceeding with caution whenever demographic goals are at stake.

Regardless of whether protagonists advocate policies to increase or diminish numbers, both must be distinguished from a position that rejects demographically motivated interventions, whatever their alleged benefits. This last position has three distinct yet mutually supportive strands. On the one hand are ethical arguments, which assume two main forms. First, there are libertarian or liberal approaches that deem it illegitimate for the state to interfere in people's private lives. Their proponents might acknowledge threats from uncontrolled population growth yet still hold that they are overridden by the dangers of political intervention (including those of extending state power). Second are post-colonial arguments, by which intervention is rejected on the grounds that 'the population problem' does not reflect real biophysical conditions but is, rather, a discursive construction grounded in colonial power relations.[1] These ethical objections are discussed in the next chapter. On the other hand there is a view that markets are better at generating optimal demographic outcomes than states, and carry fewer political risks. Because this latter strand of the non-interventionist position is still interested in demographic outcomes, it is explained below.

The demographic context

An important characteristic of population growth is that it occurs exponentially, such that apparently small growth rates (say, 2 per cent per annum) produce counter-intuitively large increases (in this case, doubling every 35 years). The larger the population, the more substantial its total becomes with each doubling. Following millennia of extremely slow increase, the growth rate started to increase significantly, first in Europe and then elsewhere, from the mid-eighteenth century. It took until 1804 for the world to acquire a billion, but a second billion had appeared by 1927 and a third by 1960. Calls for population control emerged amidst anxieties about a population explosion. Fortunately, negative feedback loops – that is, countervailing tendencies that suppress potential growth rates – have foreclosed the kind of staggering figures occasionally computed. The growth rate is slowing, having declined from 1.24 per cent p.a. in 2005 to 1.10 per cent in 2017, although this still yields some 83 million additional bodies each year.

The United Nations publishes *World Population Prospects* biennially. Drawing on country censuses and samples, it updates existing trends and revises future projections. Projections are not predictions but estimates, based on extrapolating from current trends and making plausible assumptions about their likely development. Uncertainty is reflected in the presentation of three principal variants, the medium version being the most widely cited and probable, but with the high and low variants also possible. Although variations in life expectancy and age composition also affect projected totals, the key difference between variants is the fertility rate: merely an average plus or minus half a child per woman over her lifetime. The medium-variant projection is predicated on an assumption that, worldwide, TFRs will converge at around replacement level (having risen slightly in the 83 lowest-fertility countries that currently exhibit sub-replacement rates). In 2010–15, the world TFR stood at 2.5, but this includes a rate of 4.3 in the 48 least developed, mainly African, countries (growing at 2.4 per cent per annum, with projected population doubling by 2050). Africa's 2017 population of 1.26 billion is projected to reach 4 billion by 2100, with some nations experiencing three- or even fivefold increases, although a list of the nine countries where population growth is likely to be concentrated also includes India, Pakistan and the United States.

The 2017 revision holds with 95 per cent certainty that in 2100, world population will lie between 9.6 and 13.2 billion. Yet this range is substantial and the total has been increased in every revision since 2002. Should expected fertility decline falter, the high variant (16.5 billion by 2100) could transpire. On the other hand, should the world TFR fall more dramatically than anticipated, there is a reasonable chance of world population plateauing or even declining during the current century. This low-variant trajectory (equating to population stabilization) is to all intents and purposes the demographic goal supported by the international community. Its advantage is that the sooner population peaks, the lower the peak will be. Based on 2017 estimates, a peak of 8.8 billion mid-century could fall to 7.3 billion by 2100.

What is needed for this to occur? The main theoretical framework within which such issues are debated is demographic transition theory. This is the closest the discipline of demography comes to having an overarching narrative or model, and it is the basis for the UN's relatively optimistic projections. In essence, the theory models a process of demographic change that is contemporaneous with and integral to modernization, from high mortality and fertility to low mortality and fertility. Falling mortality (especially infant mortality) is identified as the catalyst of transition because this disrupts a relatively stable (pre-industrial) condition in which births and deaths are in equilibrium. Mortality decline rather than fertility increase is the trigger for unprecedented rates of population growth as living standards rise. Crucially, transition theory predicts that further modernization will result in fertility decline, although this is typically a more protracted process. The time lag between the two phases dictates how rapidly and for how long numbers will continue to rise. This is the most critical period for policy interventions but also the most challenging since efforts to curtail fertility usually begin at a stage of development when unpropitious cultural values (pro-natalist, patriarchal) incite resistance, while state capacities remain rudimentary. Nonetheless, and despite acknowledging national variations, the theory maintains that the modernizing forces that cause mortality decline eventually instigate fertility decline, too. Growth persists for a while because of the momentum from previous high-fertility cohorts, but the theoretical expectation is that numbers will eventually stabilize as fertility and mortality return to equilibrium (with a TFR around 2.1). Although this occurs at a far higher level than before transition, the assumption is that modernization will have engendered the technological advances needed to support it.

Demographic transition theory rarely figures in political scientists' discussions, yet the role of the state in bringing transitions about is an important issue for consideration. Critics complain that the theory encourages complacency, inasmuch as it takes the form of a Eurocentric, teleological narrative in which worldwide modernization and development – now spearheaded by globalization – appear to guarantee universal completion of the process. While past transitions provide substantial evidential support, the critical question is whether future transitions will necessarily follow the same path. Political decisions and state competencies are among the contingent variables affecting outcomes.

Alongside economic development, governments' biopolitical interventions play an important role in triggering transition, for example through changing everyday habits pertaining to health, diet and childcare in ways conducive to lower mortality. But are such micro-level interventions not equally important in the next phase, that of fertility transition? Ensuring high-quality family planning services and instilling a small family norm are among the political factors that determine the course of transition. The UN presents even its medium-variant projection as a goal requiring 'substantial reductions in fertility', for which 'it will be essential to support continued improvements in access to reproductive health-care services, including family planning'.[2] Processes like economic development, women's empowerment and social security systems that reduce dependence on relatives have historically discouraged large families indirectly, by disincentivizing high-order births. They, too, rely on good governance and political choices. This suggests that political contingencies play a significant role during transition. It is difficult to say how decisive state involvement is for completion. But arguably it has played a vital part in accomplishing previous transitions and it appears to perform this role especially effectively when it pursues welfare policies mobilized, inter alia, by demographic goals.

Arguments for stabilizing and/or reducing human numbers

Demographic trends do not in and of themselves set population goals, but they do suggest and inform them. Attempts are sometimes made to estimate an optimum (usually greatly reduced) world population, but such a figure is usually judged incalculable and efforts to maintain it impracticable or unethical. This does not, however, preclude identifying a beneficial direction of travel. Some technological optimists maintain that Earth can accommodate an indefinite number of people. More common is acknowledgement that stabilizing growth sooner rather than later would have overwhelmingly positive effects: for social, gender, global and intergenerational justice; for development prospects; for natural ecosystems. While there are national variations, at world level disagreement mainly hinges on whether a slowing growth trend demonstrates the inevitability of stabilization, or whether this needs to be helped along by government interventions and an international political will to act.

The development argument

When summarizing its 2017 projections, the UN alludes to a development rationale for reducing fertility rates: rapid population growth harms the prospects of the world's poorest nations and is not therefore in their interests. Specifically, it makes it harder for their governments 'to eradicate poverty, reduce inequality, combat hunger and malnutrition, expand and update education and health systems, improve the provision of basic services and ensure that no one is left behind'.[3]

The causal (chicken-and-egg) relationship between population growth and development has been a contentious matter for population politics. Conventional modernization theory holds that as nations develop, their fertility rates decline due to factors like lower infant mortality and cultural modernization, which respectively reduce incentives for numerous births while making birth control more acceptable. The Indian delegation to the UN's first intergovernmental World Population Conference (Bucharest, 1974) expressed the idea pithily: development is the best form of contraception. Post-war research, however, reversed this causal relationship. High fertility was now held responsible for a low-equilibrium 'Malthusian trap' in which large families preclude the capital accumulation needed for economic take-off. This suggested that reproductive technologies could be an effective way to spring the trap of underdevelopment. Critics regarded this as a quick fix that ignores the real causes of underdevelopment, namely unequal trade arrangements and inadequate support for broader development strategies. The argument was nevertheless influential during the post-war decades and a perception that high fertility – associated with rapid population growth and a high dependency ratio – impedes development persists, as testified by the UN's 2017 summary.

A decade earlier, a British parliamentary report, *Return of the Population Growth Factor: Its Impact upon the Millennium Development Goals* (2007), had been something of an outlier in reminding audiences that historically no country has developed sufficiently to eliminate poverty without first reducing its fertility rate. It lamented that while 'experts agree that world population growth poses serious threats to human health, socio-economic development, and the environment', population issues had lost priority relative to other development factors. Aspiring to reverse this trend, the report offered an evidence-based assessment of the impact of population growth on Millennium Development Goals (MDGs), with a summary update in 2009 reiterating its conclusion that while MDGs would prove difficult or impossible to achieve with existing levels of population increase, greater investment in voluntary family planning programmes could significantly contribute to development priorities like climate change, failed states and poverty alleviation.[4]

The report is indicative of a growing tendency to

merge development and environmental rationales for population stabilization within a framework of sustainable development. Persistent population growth is identified, here, as an obstacle to both poverty relief and ecological integrity. A 2013 report by the UN's Sustainable Development Solutions Network (SDSN) exemplifies this renewed tendency to include demographic factors among the causes of unsustainability.

> High fertility rates raise overall population growth rates, reduce the growth rate of income per capita, and greatly impede the eradication of extreme poverty. High population growth can put unmanageable demands on the natural environment, leading, for example, to excessive water use, habitat destruction, and loss of biodiversity. High fertility rates also increase the risk of insecurity by exacerbating poverty, youth unemployment, and migration within and across countries.[5]

Both these reports call for the development of a new framework for advocating population stabilization within a human rights framework, that is, one in which collective demographic ends are compatible with ethical means.

The environmental argument

There now exists considerable evidence that planet Earth is facing a multifaceted environmental crisis. This need not in itself signal a need to control human population. But to the extent that expanding numbers make a significant contribution, reducing them becomes a rational part of mitigation (and adaptation) strategies. As with development, it is difficult to establish relative causalities. The UN summarizes the problem: while 'general trends of rapid population growth, sustained but uneven development and environmental degradation are generally well accepted', the causal relationships between them are complex and less well understood. Even so, they are understood sufficiently to suggest that, alongside other remedies, 'early stabilization of the world population would be a crucial contribution towards the achievement of sustainable development.'[6] Simon Caney's capacious definition of the environment is useful here because it alludes to the complexity of the earth system. It is 'the natural world including the earth's lithosphere (the earth's crust) and pedosphere (its soil) and the natural resources contained therein, the atmosphere, the hydrosphere and the biosphere.'[7] In the Anthropocene – a new geological epoch characterized by the indelible effects of human activity on the earth system – change occurs across all these levels, through innumerable human–non-human interfaces. While theorists are reflecting upon its implications for normative ideas about human exceptionalism, the material connection between more people and anthropogenic (i.e. human-caused) environmental change is an important consideration too.

While few environmentalists claim that a burgeoning human population is the sole, or even the principal, cause of unsustainability, it is increasingly accepted as a significant yet malleable factor. 'The size of the human population is not the only variable stressing Earth. But it is a powerful force that is also eminently amenable to change, if the international political will can be mustered.'[8] Biodiversity loss is an obvious area where population size is important because the habitat lost to other species is closely related to humans' spatial proliferation across the earth. Space (land) is one of the more manifestly limited resources and it is increasingly colonized by sprawling urban developments and infrastructure, as well as by the extensive hinterlands needed to service them. Mass extinctions and declines among non-human populations are among well-documented casualties. For biocentric thinkers and deep ecologists especially, this is reason enough to reduce human numbers. But across all dimensions of environmental degradation, the basic point is that while production, consumption and demography are inseparable, population is a multiplier.

Population size is important because it amplifies harmful per capita impacts. Impacts are unevenly distributed, and distributive justice remains a massive political challenge. But within any context, the combined effect of individuals' unsustainable activities is magnified by their number. The IPAT formula (in which Impact = Population × Affluence × Technology) nicely signals the relationship between key elements while also accommodating their co-variability over time and place. While the nature and extent of harmful impacts from population expansion vary geographically, efforts at increasing social justice are themselves hampered by rising numbers. This realization is captured in the maxim that all social and environmental problems become more difficult, and ultimately impossible, to resolve with ever more people. The underlying proposition is simple: supporting an increasingly large and affluent population on a planet with finite resources is detrimental not only to the planet's biophysical fabric but also to the texture of social relations. Efforts at achieving global equality, universally decent living standards and intergenerational justice are all impeded by ever more people.

Numbers, then, multiply ecological footprints. Collectively, these footprints have already exceeded Earth's carrying capacity. At 2013 consumption rates, the Global Footprint Network calculates that the equivalent of 1.7 Earths is needed to sustain us. While poor people have the smallest footprints, the impact of multiplying small damaging activities (like deforestation), especially when coupled with justified aspirations to develop (and to achieve living standards better than those that simply satisfy basic needs), is not insubstantial. Meanwhile, an increasing number of eco-debtors is dependent on a diminishing number of eco-creditors (that is, peoples who still live sustainably within their territory's natural capacity to support them). Satisfaction of their abundant desires relies on global trade and a worldwide distribution of environmental risk. Even so, we are collectively drawing on natural capital stocks faster than they can be replenished. Everyone's prospects are jeopardized (including those of other species and vulnerable communities) by planetary overshoot, as epitomized by climate change. The situation is sometimes summarized as a 'perfect storm'.

> If we think of the entire biosphere as essential to production, then the destruction in it that is

> associated with population growth is bound to act back on our capacity to produce. This is the apparently irremovable reason why more people are going to mean more misery. It is the destruction of soils and forests, amounting in large areas to desertification, the shortage of water and the pollution of what is left, the loss of biological diversity, the temperature and other changes in the atmosphere . . . , that today are seen by the experts in the relevant sciences as setting insurmountable limits to the number of people who are able to live (let alone to live well) in particular countries and on the planet as a whole.[9]

Reducing the footprints of wealthier consumers is often endorsed as a fairer alternative to population control. It would certainly help. Yet consuming more, rather than less, seems to be an almost universal ambition. Indeed, global capitalism (sanitized in official reports as the unsustainable business-as-usual model) is inherently reliant on sustained economic growth, which requires it constantly to incite new appetites and open new markets. A fast-growing global middle class is enthusiastically embracing conspicuous consumption, an ideal propagated through advertising and the media. It is comforting to believe that new technologies will square the circle, but meanwhile a new generation of sceptics is renewing a more radical solution that focuses on limits and boundaries. Rather than addressing shortages and degradations by continuously increasing supply (mainstream economists' preference), they call for reductions in personal demand and in the number of demanders: a comprehensive overhaul of business-as-usual and its consumerist values not as an alternative to, but in tandem with, population stabilization.

Such thinking is reminiscent of, and avowedly indebted to, an earlier limits-to-growth thesis. Research for the iconic *Limits to Growth* (1972) was undertaken at MIT, where scientists working under the aegis of the Club of Rome used new computing capabilities to model future scenarios. These were based on five sub-systems, of which population and industrial production were accorded greatest significance. Each sub-system was quantified, using data from long-term trends and assumptions about their likely trajectory, 1900–2100. Trends manifesting an internal momentum towards 'super-exponential' growth were found to be driving the earth system (labelled *Gaia* by James Lovelock) to exceed critical thresholds of system maintenance. As positive feedback loops acquired unstoppable but unpredictable momentum, even scenarios incorporating plausible technological innovations manifested increasing volatility followed by collapse. The core problem was identified as exponential growth in a complex, finite system. An updated rerun of the MIT programme in 1992 yielded similar, if even more alarming, results. The only scenario avoiding systemic breakdown was population stabilization and a steady-state economy. *Limits to Growth* equates this sustainable society with fewer people, using intermediate technologies, resulting in their enjoying more leisure and a higher quality of life despite less consumption and reproduction. This image of the good life was mirrored in contemporaneous critiques of consumer capitalism in 'overdeveloped' societies, by New Left thinkers such as Herbert Marcuse in his *Essay on Liberation* (1972).[10]

Following decades of vitriolic attacks on the limits thesis, Andrew Dobson has recently identified a 'recognizable second wave of limits to growth thinking'.[11] This is illustrated by the Royal Society's *People and the Planet* (2012), a report that celebrated the fortieth anniversary of *Limits* by endorsing its conclusion: that 'a gradual and equitable decline in numbers will serve humanity best', especially if complemented by reductions in material consumption by the better-off and by 'changes to the current economic model' of persistent economic growth.[12]

The planetary boundaries approach developed by Johan Rockström is another influential example of this second wave. While they focus on making a positive estimation of the safe operating spaces for human development, rather than emphasizing limits, Rockström and his colleagues also endorse their predecessors' core message: that the 'exponential growth of human activities is raising concern that further pressure on the earth system could destabilize critical biophysical systems and trigger abrupt or irreversible environmental changes that would be deleterious or even catastrophic for human well-being.'[13] They acknowledge that setting the boundaries of acceptable risk in situations of uncertainty requires societies to make normative judgements, but they also insist that choices be informed by understanding non-subjective thresholds.

This is the approach applied by the team, co-chaired by Rockström, in *An Action Agenda for Sustainable Development* (2013). Its remit was technical advice for setting the Sustainable Development Goals (SDGs) that would replace the MDGs from 2015. The report notes that profound material changes since 2000 include a 'drastically higher human impact on the physical Earth' that 'will expand dangerously without an urgent and radical change of course'. Under current technological conditions, the world economy is already exceeding several planetary boundaries. Coupled with projected population increases, 'unprecedented crises of food production, public health, and natural disasters' are probable. Its advice prioritizes 'decelerating population growth more rapidly' in order to speed up stabilization. If this recommendation was omitted from the actual SDGs, this is indicative of a hiatus that currently exists, in which scientific studies are increasingly including population stabilization among their policy goals, yet the toxic legacy of population control deters policy makers from explicitly endorsing it.

Studies that model the impact of bigger populations on specific sustainability variables are a further indication of new 'limits-to-growth' approaches. In the case of greenhouse gas emissions, additional individual emitters are shown not only to multiply the harm each causes, but also to negate any benefit from per capita cuts. A 2017 study finds that having one child fewer is by far the most effective lifestyle option for limiting personal emissions.[14] Modelling the cumulative impact of descendants as a carbon legacy of current fertility choices shows that potential savings from reduced reproduction greatly exceed any saving from lifestyle changes.

Similar arguments address food supplies, where an estimated 70 per cent increase in production is needed to feed the 2050 population. While official reports tend to be cautiously optimistic that more efficient agriculture, using new biotechnologies, can prevent famine, a more radical option – of reducing total demand through 'lowering our numbers globally – noncoercively, through the exercise of reproductive rights' – is gaining traction.[15]

In summary, reducing numbers emerges from recent studies as one of the most effective and practicable ways of improving resource security, reducing negative externalities and generating conditions conducive to achieving equal life chances. Safe, reliable and accessible reproductive technology, when used voluntarily, emerges as the cheapest and most user-friendly technology available for ensuring intergenerational justice and sustainable development. The point about these conclusions is not that they call for 'coercive population control', but, rather, that they provide an objective environmental rationale for prioritizing universal provision of comprehensive family planning services in order to stabilize world numbers as quickly as is feasible through voluntary means.

This demographic dimension nonetheless remains a taboo among many green members of environmentalism's social movement wing, for whom achieving social justice is paramount and reversing population growth is considered a racist, post-colonial strategy. Yet, as argued earlier, population growth may be a significant contributor to persistent poverty and inequality. While, moreover, suppressing consumption is their preferred ecological strategy because it focuses demands for change on wealthier peoples, this does not rule out an appreciation of the benefits of reducing population growth in developed countries. When the Brundtland Report put the concept of sustainable development centre-stage in 1987, it recognized that the accumulation of people in 'overdeveloped' countries is disproportionately hazardous because a 'child born in a country where levels of material and energy use are high places a greater burden on the Earth's resources than a child born in a poorer country'.[16] These post-transitional nations currently exhibit low, mainly sub-replacement, fertility rates but large ecological footprints. The environmental advantages of allowing their populations naturally to dwindle – say, to mid-twentieth-century levels – is rarely, however, mentioned, even though this is arguably where a non-interventionist population policy could be most environmentally helpful.[17] Indeed, with interests in economic growth and national security having engendered a new pronatalism, there is scope for progressive thinkers to develop a robust critique of such policies and of the business-as-usual model they support.

The existential argument

So far, the focus has been on the disadvantages of rapid population growth (for development) and the expansion of absolute numbers (for the environment). Discussions about the impact of higher-density living on everyday existence are less frequent as they concern more 'subjective' judgements about quality of life. This is an area where political theorists could make a distinctive contribution, reviving a tradition of reflecting on the good life that has recently been discouraged by deontological and multiculturalist objections. Here they can draw on objective studies that find that everyday connectedness with living green things enhances well-being, while crowded conditions are associated with poor mental and physical health. A utopian tradition provides a rich archive describing relatively small communities living harmoniously with the natural world. Conversely, dystopias are routinely associated with crowded, technologically engineered habitats in which lives are alienated from vital forces and natural pleasures. Critics may interpret these recurrent images as simple nostalgia but on our packed, urbanized planet they resonate with happiness and grief.

This resonance is memorably expressed by a digression in J. S. Mill's *Principles of Political Economy* (1848). Mill acknowledged that modern economies could probably support larger numbers but doubted this would mean 'a better or a happier population' and confessed, 'I see very little reason for desiring it.'[18] He poses a provocative question to proponents of continuous expansion: *why* should sustained economic and demographic growth be considered beneficial (and beneficial for whom?), once certain levels of material well-being and critical mass have been achieved? Among the casualties of sustained growth, Mill describes a natural environment with 'every flowery waste or natural pasture ploughed up, all quadrupeds or birds which are not domesticated for man's use exterminated as his rivals for food'. He opines that 'a world from which solitude is extirpated, is a very poor ideal' and laments a future in which population growth eliminates spaces where unregulated life or experiences of the non-human occur.[19] As sustainable development addresses global food and energy needs by covering the countryside with genetically modified crops, glass and plastic, wind turbines and solar panels, Mill's question surely remains pertinent. Is it desirable that humans should inhabit an entirely anthropocentric environment, reduced to 'ecological services' for their life support? It is a valid point that there are diverse conceptions of the good life, but who celebrates the prospect of a silent spring? When the Brundtland Report conceded the inevitability of further population growth, it recommended nurturing resilience through helping people adjust to 'problems of overcrowding and excessive population densities' by teaching the 'tolerance and empathy required for living in a crowded world'.[20] The aim is worthy but what it counsels is adaptation to an impoverished, stressful condition.

Social as well as natural ecologies are compromised by rising densities. Over half the world's people are now urban dwellers. In fast-growing cities everywhere, the multiplying effect of population on negative externalities is amplified by the impact of rising densities on everyday lives. Once lauded for the excitement its vibrant spaces afforded the cosmopolitan *flâneur*, the metropolis has become a mega-city characterized by polluted air, traffic congestion, crowded or privatized public spaces, loss of green or marginal lands, deficient services and housing shortages. The artists that enliven and regenerate urban landscapes, and the key workers that service them, are driven out for lack of affordable space. Rising numbers are not the only culprit, but their contribution is significant. Land is a finite resource and the recourse of city planners everywhere is to build more densely, usually upwards, both to accommodate more people in less space and to exploit economies of scale. This may have ecological advantages over suburban sprawl, but as minimum dwelling sizes are reduced and families are increasingly housed in high-rises or concentrated in slums, it surely behoves us to ask if this is a recipe for the good life. Good design helps. But in densely populated countries like England and India (and even in the far less densely populated United States), studies repeatedly find public preferences for lower-density living, as reflected in the purchase of more space by those who can afford it.[21] In everyday lives, the adverse effects of overcrowding are less well researched, yet they permeate mundane routines and increase the stresses of surviving in conditions where there is constant competition for scarce resources, a game of musical chairs where there is never enough to go around.

Critical mass has economic advantages, although without necessarily benefiting all or most individuals. Beyond a certain density, however, diseconomies of scale also desynchronize supply and demand. Systems must be continuously scaled up just to maintain the per capita status quo. Where rising demand for infrastructure is addressed, cities may become permanent building sites with no net benefit to most inhabitants. Austerity measures certainly exacerbate experiences of public service deficits and infrastructure running at over-capacity, but research reveals deeper structural problems. Using full economic accounting (which includes the costs of externalities), Jane O'Sullivan shows how the burdens of population growth on public assets are routinely underestimated and therefore skew cost–benefit analyses in a pro-growth direction.[22] Although a growing population usually increases GDP, and hence tax revenues, merely maintaining durable assets and services at existing levels requires disproportionately higher levels of investment. Research suggests that a ratio of at least 12.5 per cent investment is needed for every 1 per cent of population growth. Hidden privatized costs of capacity shortfalls are meanwhile quietly borne by individuals who suffer deteriorating health and well-being.

Reflection on thickening densities and on the good life in an increasingly crowded world may, in conclusion, be overdue. Explaining adverse urban experiences as a cost of crowding is controversial, especially inasmuch as it touches on immigration and vested economic interests. This need not, however, produce a discourse that 'blames' new arrivals for deficits. Rather, and regardless of particular contributions to aggregate wealth (GDP), it calls for consideration of the diverse ways in which everyone's experiences and life chances are harmed when everyone is competing over diminishing spaces. This includes the fate of those inhabiting the unplanned slum settlements that UN-HABITAT fears will become the dominant urban form in developing regions.

Economic arguments for and against demographic intervention

Economists are interested in demographic change because it affects resources and productivity. They are especially interested in a particular population, namely the workforce, regarding its reproduction, skills and size relative to other (dependent) sections of the population. Economists occupy the full range of positions outlined at the beginning of this chapter. Depending on circumstances, they may favour either increasing or diminishing numbers as a demographic goal. Since orthodox theory holds that market forces will match demographic trends to economic requirements, they mostly however reject state intervention. There are two recent schools of thought that bear on this matter. The first is indebted to Adam Smith when it asserts that where overpopulation (relative to employment opportunities) does occur, an invisible hand will restore equilibrium by incentivizing lower fertility and/or higher economic growth. The second is more interventionist in that it encourages policy makers to simulate economic discipline in circumstances where markets fail. This is exemplified by today's ageing, post-transitional societies, where low fertility associated with labour shortages and falling productivity has engendered support for the 'new pro-natalism' and positive net migration.

In the first case, markets are attributed capacities to realize an ideal IPAT equilibrium. In its current manifestation, this argument combines neoliberal economics with rational choice theory. It gained ascendancy during the 1980s, when it was used explicitly to condemn anti-natalist population control policies. The prevailing neo-Malthusian orthodoxy was disputed on the one hand by questioning whether population growth really is disadvantageous for development, and on the other by insisting that even in situations where fertility decline may be beneficial, it is best served by economic rather than political pressures. Political intervention was not only deemed unnecessary but accused of actually harming the economic imperatives that render small families a rational choice. The economist Julian Simon was particularly influential in establishing the new position, for example through his *The Economics of Population Growth* (1977).[23] Simon explicitly rejected the message of *Limits to Growth* on the grounds that output has a tendency to grow at least as fast as population and without apparent limit.

A political expression of this argument appears in the statement produced by the Reagan Administration for the 1984 ICPD in Mexico City. It denies that more people necessarily mean less growth; whether they are an asset or a burden depends on labour market conditions. On the one hand, it maintains, these conditions are harmed by 'economic statism'; on the other, the remedy for overpopulation is deregulated markets, which function as a 'natural mechanism' for slowing growth. This 'controlling factor' is understood as 'the adjustment, by individual families, of reproductive behavior to economic opportunity and aspiration'. The argument had tangible political effects: US development aid was redirected from family planning into programmes supporting economic progress 'through encouraging sound economic policies and freeing of individual initiative', especially in the private sector.[24] At the same time, support was withdrawn from any organization supporting abortion, a policy reinstated by every Republican president since.

The claim that economic freedom engenders rational fertility choices follows from assumptions that reproductive decisions are subjected to cost–benefit analysis and numerous children are expensive. The idea of a 'natural' homeostatic mechanism draws on rational choice theories initially expounded by members of the Chicago School. Gary Becker and Peter Bauer explicitly applied their arguments to reproductive decision making. As children become economic burdens, as the quality of offspring (their human capital) trumps their quantity in contributing to the household economy and as the need for a dual-earner family heaps financial pressures on child rearing, the calculation is that rational individuals will 'freely' choose small families. This faith in systemic equilibrium marks a fundamental disagreement with limits and boundaries positions, which predict systemic disequilibrium and collapse unless pro-growth, market-oriented economies are fundamentally transformed.

While deregulated markets are accorded powers to suppress fertility where it impedes development, overall economists favour larger, rising populations, regarding them as an engine of prosperity. This is reflected in mainstream policy making, which mainly accepts Simon's argument that more people mean a bigger market and workforce, a larger reservoir of ingenuity and, where population pressures do occur, more revenues to alleviate them. This is sometimes supplemented by the Environmental Kuznets Curve, a theory that expects ecological damage caused during industrial development to be repaired as richer, better-educated people nurture their environments, while their consumer demands level off. Although there is little evidence to support the curve (for example regarding consumption or greenhouse gas emissions) and its presumptions are widely criticized, economists expect markets to incentivize high-tech 'green growth' with similarly beneficial effects.[25] 'Decoupling' economic growth from natural resource use (for example through resource substitutions and a 'weightless' economy) is the holy grail of sustainable economic growth.

Economists mainly oppose population control, then, both because they expect market forces to synchronize demographic outcomes with economic requirements and because, overall, they equate population growth and size with prosperity. As long as populations continue naturally to increase, they are happy to embrace this as a default position while criticizing measures to suppress fertility rates. Here they are joined by other constituencies ranged against anti-natalist population controls. Religious conservatives usually oppose anti-natalism on the grounds that manipulating a natural, God-given process of life creation is an expression of human hubris that is disrespectful of human lives and disruptive of family bonds. The Catholic Church regards not only abortion but also contraception as sinful, with the Vatican playing a particularly active role in opposing population control. Since around 1980, the melding of neoliberal economics and socially conservative values in the American New Right has created a powerful obstacle to proponents of limits to growth and population stabilization policies.

A more sympathetic attitude towards population growth is also appearing within emerging economies like China (which introduced a two-child policy in 2017) and India (where neoliberalism has gained traction since 1991). This is partly explained by their advance through demographic transition. Transition theory explains that, as fertility rates fall, countries are rewarded with a 'demographic dividend', a 'window' that temporarily opens as the last large cohorts of children move into working age. This stage can be disastrous if employment opportunities are insufficient or potential workers lack the human capital to exploit them. But if economic conditions are propitious, a low dependency ratio and higher revenues can intensify development for a period, especially if it follows an industrial pathway that exploits and soaks up plentiful cheap labour (as exemplified by China). While this route is particularly environmentally damaging, a more sustainable hi-tech alternative generates far fewer jobs – a problem when numbers are still rising through population momentum and labour markets must expand simply to absorb them. In either case, it is important to remember that the dividend is not a reason for celebrating population growth but a reward for fertility decline. Its benefits arise less from high numbers per se than from a low dependency ratio that is necessarily transient, a precursor to population ageing.

As the working-age bulge ages further and retires, the dependency ratio rises again. Labour shortages and fiscal problems emerge as the working-age population declines relative to other age cohorts. Fertility decline plus increasing life expectancy produces population ageing as the last phase of transition. Population ageing is a predictable phase of late transition, but although older populations are likely to remain the norm, today's unbalanced age profiles will largely be ameliorated once baby boomers die and are replaced by a smaller, more age-balanced population (closer to the post-transitional equilibrium predicted by transition theory). The situation becomes acute temporarily (for around four decades), however, in countries where a low-fertility baby-boom generation is retiring, a situation attributed, ironically, to the success of market discipline in disincentivizing its reproduction. Very low fertility rates may be a harbinger of actual decline.

This is where a second school of economic thinking becomes apparent, as demographic interventions are encouraged in order to compensate for markets' failure to incentivize sufficient workforce renewal. Population ageing (and even more so decline) is inimical to economic orthodoxy because it is equated with falling productivity and GDP. Older people are not just regarded as unproductive dependants (although strenuous efforts are being made to keep them in the workforce); their care needs also make them expensive. Labour shortages are further associated with rising wages. In a competitive global economy, ageing societies are regarded as disadvantaged compared with youthful competitors enjoying a demographic dividend. Pro-natalist policy interventions are accordingly advocated, the aim being to raise the median age and produce a new generation of workers. From this point of view, immigration is actually preferable since migrants are more likely to arrive skilled-up and of working age. The political right generally prefers pro-natalism as it coincides with pro-life, pro-family (and nativist) social conservativism. But for most economists, pro-natalism and positive net migration are simply pragmatic responses to sub-optimal demographic trends, especially where fertility decline has overshot its expected stabilization at replacement level (in a phenomenon sometimes referred to as a second demographic transition).

There are alternative policy options for addressing population ageing, such as linking the retirement age to life expectancy, pension reform and 'active ageing' programmes. But demographic interventions whose aim is to synthesize conditions akin to the demographic dividend are widespread.[26] From a demographic perspective, the problem with the immigration solution is that migrants also age. Unless a nation is committed to sustained population growth, it merely delays returning to a more balanced age profile. Numbers are indeed projected to expand considerably in most post-transition nations (the United States, Australia, the United Kingdom, France, etc.), as recovering birth rates and substantial immigration respond to pro-growth policy initiatives. The pro-natalist option also has drawbacks (such as expensive childcare subsidies to incentivize larger families, further increasing the dependency ratio and, where successful, restoring natural population growth), although it has been seized upon by many post-transitional governments since the 1990s.[27]

Pro-natalist policies are not usually considered population control, or judged coercive, because their supporters tend to regard them as somehow attuned to life and to women's natural proclivities and because, as currently deployed, policies are framed in feminist terms and are directed at individuals' choice architecture where they remain largely invisible. Yet inasmuch as the state steps in to raise fertility rates, its goal of modifying reproductive conduct – in order to achieve wider demographic and thence economic ends – mirrors neo-Malthusian endeavours in the opposite direction. As chapter 3 shows, current models of governance offer a similar repertoire of measures to both sides; the main difference is the political choice of which goal to pursue. Critics of policies for rejuvenating population growth argue that GDP is a poor measure of economic performance since it ignores externalities (including unpriced costs to natural capital and personal well-being), while its rise does not necessarily increase per capita incomes. In this latter case, it is important to identify winners and losers, with low-waged and less skilled people being particularly disadvantaged. Conversely, lower GDP does not automatically equate to poorer individuals because smaller populations make fewer demands on social and ecological services. Indeed, incomes and well-being may be enhanced, provided that decline occurs at a pace at which excessive infrastructure is scaled down gradually. This is especially the case if labour shortages increase wages directly, or if they incentivize technological innovations that increase individual productivity and raise wages indirectly.

Japan presents an interesting case study because it exhibits the greatest population ageing and has already passed peak population. Concerted pro-natalist efforts have borne little fruit but immigration is not favoured. Instead, there is substantial investment in AI-enhanced robots that will replace or enhance workers and care for the elderly. *Contra* Simon, Japan shows labour shortages driving innovation. In fact, workforces everywhere are increasingly being replaced by intelligent machines. From this perspective, it is not only environmentally dangerous to increase affluent populations; it is also short-sighted to inflate labour forces, just as entire populations look destined to become surplus to labour-market requirements and deprived of a living wage. This new technology looks certain to affect both the business-as-usual model and demographic trends, although it is difficult to predict how. Perhaps an existential crisis, sometimes predicted as a consequence of joblessness, will encourage people to have more children in an effort to give meaning to their lives; perhaps it will discourage them from breeding at all.

Conclusion

To summarize the theoretical field outlined in this chapter: the issue of controlling numbers as a policy objective harbours several positions. A preference for demographic controls may favour either population stabilization/reduction or population retention/growth. Either might or might not use coercive means. Both are to be distinguished from rejections of public intervention that are typically motivated by distrust of state interference in the private sphere. Some exponents of this last position express faith in market forces to optimize demographic trends through calibrating reproductive choices. For most orthodox economists, population growth is welcome and a new enthusiasm for state intervention has emerged in so far as public policy can increase numbers wherever stabilization or decline look likely. Inversely, for those who do recognize advantages to stabilizing world numbers, devising policy mechanisms to achieve voluntary fertility reduction has become a political and ethical imperative. Where fertility is already below replacement, on the other hand, inaction would be the best option, although at the moment population policy is rarely discussed in these terms.

Since voluntarism is widely understood as the antithesis of coercion, and this opposition has become the principal terrain on which normative disagreements over population control are fought, the next two chapters examine respectively charges that its means are morally reprehensible and practically coercive.

2

The Ethics of Population Control: Reproductive Freedom and Human Rights

The previous chapter was written from a consequentialist perspective, where disagreements about the direction and efficacy of population policies hinge on the merits of pursuing particular demographic goals. The extent to which collective outcomes are the primary or sole criterion for political decision making depends, however, upon prior ethical commitments. For liberals who maintain a strict division between the public and private realms, for those who believe that certain natural or human rights are absolute and non-negotiable, from a Kantian perspective for which autonomous moral agents must never be used instrumentally as means to external ends, consequentialist approaches to population control rest on flawed moral premises, regardless of the utility of outcomes or the mechanisms deployed.

This chapter assesses these normative arguments, whose criteria are ethical and political rather than environmental and demographic. They draw on classical liberal (and postclassical neoliberal) arguments about individuals' freedom to make choices about their private lives and to be the best judge of their own interests. They include objections to utilitarian consequentialism, whose commitment to maximizing aggregate happiness is associated with expedient calculations that may override some individuals' rights. This is in turn connected to broader debates about the distinctive nature of politics, as a strategic field of power relations in which the connections between means and ends differ from those espoused by moralists. These disputes have been rehearsed among political thinkers since Machiavelli. They have occasionally been applied explicitly to the population question and they continue to underpin current disagreements about the legitimacy of state interference in reproductive decisions. In a nutshell: do individual freedom, autonomy, privacy and rights preclude population control, or do adverse collective impacts from unregulated procreation sometimes justify public action, in which case how much latitude should it be accorded?

Classical liberal arguments about freedom are explored in the first part of this chapter. The core question here is whether, and if so under what circumstances, it is permissible for governments to interfere with reproductive liberty. Given population policies' interest in modifying fertility behaviour, it is unsurprising that such arguments should have acquired particular resonance for feminists, for whom reproductive rights are central to women's emancipation, empowerment and equality. Human, and in particular reproductive, rights arguments against population control are discussed in the second part of the chapter. The key question here is whether it is (ever) legitimate for governments to tell women (or couples) how many children they may produce, or whether this violates their rights. Note that both these discussions are framed in humanist terms. Among others, Donna Haraway's work serves as a reminder of the 'human exceptionalism' embedded in most human rights discourse (although the rights framework is itself sometimes applied to animals and other natural entities when legal protection and respect are sought for non-human beings). While acknowledging that earlier population policies often perpetrated injustices, Haraway argues that it is an imperative of 'multi-species reproductive justice' that the problems caused by overpopulation are acknowledged and efforts made to reduce future numbers substantially.[1]

Reproductive freedom and collective action

A good place to start is J. S. Mill's essay 'On Liberty' (1859), because it is commonly regarded as the classic defence of (negative) liberty and because Mill includes reproduction freedom in his inquiry. Mill was a social liberal who used a modified version of utilitarian reasoning. He was aware that capacities for and experiences of personal happiness depend upon the broader social context, and here he championed a pluralistic liberal culture. His essay reflects on principles for establishing the limits of justifiable incursion on freedom, and it offers a robust defence of civil liberties and individual privacy. His aim, Mill writes, is 'to assert one very simple principle': regarding sanctions through physical force in the form of legal penalties, or moral coercion exercised through public opinion, the sole end that justifies non-consensual interference is 'to prevent harm to others' (his 'harm principle'). 'Over himself, over his own body and mind,' he insists, 'the individual is sovereign.'[2]

It might be inferred that in matters as intimately corporeal as fertility, negative liberty will be sacrosanct. Jeremy Waldron convincingly explains why Mill would not have included moral distress caused by unconventional sexual behaviour under his 'harm principle', or therefore regarded this as a legitimate area for intervention.[3] Sexuality is a self-regarding act: that is, an act that affects only the individuals involved or affects others in trivial ways which they must tolerate. Mill himself objected to compulsory medical examinations for women under the Contagious Diseases Act. Conversely, acts that harm others' interests in non-trivial ways are classified as other-regarding and they may in principle be interfered with by society or state. Mill here includes responsibilities to the society that protects liberty, placing a positive duty on individuals to avoid injuring others and to bear their fair share of society's burdens. Once procreation occurs, sexual activity moves into this category of other-regarding acts.

It does not follow that such acts should automatically be subjected to public intervention. 'As soon as any part of a person's conduct affects prejudicially the interests of others, society has jurisdiction over it,' Mill asserts, 'and the question whether the general welfare will or will not be promoted by interfering with it, becomes open to discussion.'[4] Evaluating the case for intervention must include its likely efficacy, the danger of unintended negative consequences, the degree of coercion required, the strength of society's interest in the outcome and the cost of diminishing individuals' self-reliance. In short, other-regarding acts are the stuff of the public sphere. Mill's version of consequentialist ethics requires that the merits of public intervention – including the means to be used, the ends they serve and the particular circumstances in which interference might be warranted – are carefully deliberated.

He argued on many occasions that large families harm the working class by reducing real wages and impeding equality. Although his observation expresses a general truth about laws of supply and demand in market economies, the way that truth operates varies according to economic and demographic conditions. In the mid-nineteenth century, he contended, high fertility had become an unambiguously other-regarding act in old, 'over-peopled' countries like Britain, whereas in new settler societies like America, with their abundant resources and relatively scant populations, large families did not adversely harm others' interests so procreation could safely be treated as self-regarding. He ruminated on the benefits of emigration/immigration in this light, too. As a youth, Mill had been arrested for distributing illegal literature on contraception and during the course of his career he suggested various measures for reducing family size. Laws proscribing early marriage; the role of public opinion in deterring large families through 'unfavourable sentiments'; opening employment to women, in order to sublimate passion and encourage fewer progeny; working-class education, including an understanding of the laws of political economy and exposure to the disciplinary effects of labour markets: these are all mentioned as ways to inculcate responsible reproductive behaviour.

In summary, Mill's version of liberalism allows both more and less direct interventions in fertility regimes, provided they follow consideration of the ends to be achieved; a convincing case is made for the collective benefits, and individual liberties that do not substantially harm others are protected. Underlying his argument is a view that children are not merely a private good. As future citizens, they become a public resource or burden and, as such, public intervention is legitimate under certain circumstances. Because circumstances, and hence impacts, vary, he recognized that reproduction may in different times and places be classified either as self- or as other-regarding. Mill's principle thus allows for contextual flexibility that avoids moral absolutism and rigid political boundaries, while maintaining important liberal and democratic constraints on interference. He maintains a bias towards personal liberty, such that freedoms cannot be overridden by consequentialist reasoning unless significant harm is demonstrated. Where public action is warranted, it is subject to careful scrutiny. Analysis in the rest of this chapter broadly supports this circumscribed consequentialism.

When neo-Malthusianism re-emerged during the 1960s, public responsibility for limiting population growth was often justified through reference to Mill's 'harm principle', with expositions of harm being expanded to include shared social and natural ecosystems ('the commons'). Garrett Hardin's iconic essay 'The Tragedy of the Commons' (1968) may be viewed as a mid-twentieth-century update of Mill's politics, inasmuch as individual liberties and responsibilities must continuously be reassessed in relation to public goods and collective outcomes.

Hardin explains why unregulated reproduction and consumption are ruinous for the commons. The tragedy he describes is indebted to Hobbes's and Locke's social contract theories and is actually twofold. First, a combination of unregulated acquisitive individualism and high fertility yields a classic collective action problem. Everyone is disadvantaged by the outcome, yet no one has a private incentive for restraint unless others are guaranteed to exercise the same. 'Freedom in a commons brings ruin to all.'[5] Thereafter, remedial actions (discussed further in chapter 3) converge around options for rationing. While Hardin identified both economic and political mechanisms for limiting user rights (markets and progressive taxation), he acknowledged that they all incur degrees of injustice, inequality, exclusion and loss. Accordingly, 'we need to re-examine our individual freedoms to see which ones are defensible'. Like Mill, Hardin recognizes that measures are 'system sensitive'. He argues that absolute, ahistorical liberties or rights are anachronisms because 'as the human population has increased, the commons has had to be abandoned in one aspect after another.'[6] Abandonment is not a one-off event but an ongoing process, as a shrinking realm of unregulated common life is incrementally destroyed or controlled. 'Every new enclosure of the commons', Hardin observes, 'involves the infringement of somebody's personal liberty' and provokes an outcry before being accepted as necessary. He expected the next and most urgent infringement to be on people's right freely to reproduce.

Such advocates of population policies, who insist upon the other-regarding nature of procreation, recognize that acts which might be ethically unobjectionable in their own terms may nevertheless inflict considerable damage on communities once they are multiplied. Hobbes's state of nature, where unrestricted freedom results in a war of all against all, despite a common desire for peace and security, exemplifies the problem. The lesson Hobbes had drawn – that it is rational to surrender liberty to a central authority capable of imposing the beneficial outcome that eludes the disorganized multitude – was not lost on those who expressed concern about an environmental crisis caused by unrestrained reproduction and consumption. Their hope, however, was that coordination could be entrusted to democratic governments responsive to the concerns of informed citizens, who would consent to mildly coercive fiscal and legislative measures (such as disincentivizing taxes) for reducing the birth rate and embrace a culture of limits reinforced by economic (dis)incentives. This would avoid more harmful outcomes, including more stringent coercion, later.

At this point, a few genealogical comments are helpful because the ideological landscape shifted during the 1970s, and one of its effects was to redraw the line between private and public, and thus between self- and other-regarding acts. Among the areas affected, procreation was redefined as a self-regarding act and inviolable rights associated with it (extending to the unborn foetus) were increased. This reflected a wider turn, both political and methodological, from collectivist and structural to more individualist and anti-state approaches (accompanied among critical theorists by a turn from politics to ethics). As government intervention was pared back, it was deemed especially coercive within the reproductive sphere. For the Reagan Administration in 1984, 'the right of couples to determine the size of their own families' was cast in opposition to 'forcible coercion' for demographic purposes.[7] As a corresponding stress on individual rights and choices grew, the close relationship between rights and responsibilities that liberal thinkers like Mill had insisted upon dissipated.

The change was not uncontested. Paul Demeny, first editor of *Population and Development Review*, rejected the reclassification of reproductive acts by explaining that the 'birth of a child, perceived as a gain for the single family, imposes costs on all other members of the society in which it is born – costs that are not taken into account in the private decisions that determine fertility'.[8] Such critics questioned the analogy with market equilibrium and insisted that demographic externalities remain 'a legitimate object of attention for collective and, in particular, governmental action'.[9] The editorial for the *Review*'s first issue in 1975 shows how Mill's 'harm principle' was being updated by games theory, which demonstrated how even personally rational procreative decisions can yield sub-optimal outcomes. The 'sum total of individual decisions may not add up to the common good. When the aggregated private preferences and the public good in demographic matters diverge greatly, people may no longer be best served by the age-old practice of relying on spontaneous processes of social adjustment.' At this point, fertility becomes 'an explicit goal of public policy'.[10]

But the political landscape was shifting in other directions, too. As the international human rights paradigm strengthened under the Clinton Administration, new political constituencies acquired powerful voices on the population question. Among them, the International Women's Movement (IWM) had become a significant force by the 1990s. It played a major role in forging the paradigm change represented by the Cairo consensus, wherein the 'numbers game' was denounced in favour of women's reproductive health rights.

Reproductive rights as human rights

Liberalism's individualist defence of personal freedom is closely related to its protection of basic human rights. Within this theoretical framework, reproductive rights raise some specific questions. Whose rights are they? Are they already covered by the universal category of basic (fundamental) rights, in which case can gendered aspects be deduced, or are they specifically women's rights? In the context of population control, how do reproductive rights stand in relation to other rights such as the right to develop? Are reproductive rights *in principle* antithetical to political interventions in fertility choices, regardless of demographic or development outcomes? Do population policies *necessarily* violate reproductive rights? To address such questions, it is helpful to distinguish between different kinds of reproductive rights (see below). But first it is useful to understand the importance they assumed in response to charges levelled against population control programmes by the IWM. Four main objections may be identified here.

The first echoes a wider post-colonial critique of population control, which denies that there is a population problem at all. Instead, population's problematization is understood as a political construction. Proponents of this objection rarely discuss numbers or biophysical limits. Rather, they identify demographic, development and environmental discourses as discursive strategies within a global power struggle. Hardt and Negri encapsulate this judgement in *Multitude*, where they argue that most 'discussions of demographic explosions and population crises . . . are not really oriented toward either bettering the lives of the poor or maintaining a sustainable total global population in line with the capacities of the planet'. Instead, their supporters are 'concerned primarily with which social groups reproduce and which do not'.[11] Western population politics since the mid-eighteenth century is perceived to have been dominated by this colonial, eugenic logic.[12] The feminist dimension of this critique maintains that worrying about overpopulation is a way of rationalizing control over women's bodies. Betsy Hartmann exemplifies this view when she argues that the population (qua environmental) problem is an 'over-exaggerated' myth deployed to justify abusing women's rights.[13]

While this objection focuses on fertility control, with feminist critics stressing its implications for women's reproductive rights, it is relevant to mention that this constructivist, post-colonial position is applied also to a second key demographic variable, namely migration, which is addressed in similar terms. Immigration control and its justifications are opposed in this case to open borders, equated with a right to free movement. While this is too vast a topic to be considered here, it is important to appreciate the challenges it poses for national stabilization population policies inasmuch as these logically imply balanced migration (i.e. zero net gains), which social justice opponents consider immoral and economists undesirable.[14]

The implication is that it is not only unnecessary but also politically too dangerous to pursue demographic goals, given the sinister geopolitical interests and dubious morality of elites. Such concerns sound a salutary warning about the ease with which anxieties (commonly parsed as 'fear of the other') about reproduction, gender and ethnicity can be co-opted for reprehensible political purposes. The previous chapter suggested that supporting gradual population decline in developed countries might help appease critics who associate population control with genocide. But here, too, critics argue that women of colour and minorities have been targets of abusive or exclusionary fertility and migration controls justified by unwarranted demographic and economic rationalizations. On the other hand, sociologists like Nikolas Rose worry that eugenics has become a rhetorical term used to condemn every intervention in population variables, whereas 'Limiting population size for economic reasons' (and surely environmental ones, too), while not immune to criticism, 'is not the same as seeking to maximize racial fitness in the service of a biological struggle between nation-states'.[15]

Other feminist objections focus more specifically on the instrumentalist implications of consequentialist approaches to population growth. This second objection arises from a neo-Kantian injunction against using women's bodies instrumentally to achieve collective ends. It is held to transgress a 'central tenet of the international women's health movement', namely that 'women's health and rights, not macrodemographic objectives, are of paramount concern'.[16] A woman-centred focus on reproductive health means recognizing its inherent value as a way 'to empower women, and not as a means to limit population growth, save the environment, and speed economic development'.[17] Third, although feminists welcome family planning services, they argue that under population control directives these are less concerned with liberating women from unwanted pregnancies than with reinforcing structured gender inequality. Thus Sonia Corrêa reasons that 'human reproduction takes place through women's bodies. Therefore, religious and cultural institutions and the population establishment operate through existing gender systems.'[18] Policy regimes that promote fewer births may from this perspective be regarded as no less gender-biased than patriarchal institutions like the Catholic Church. In Joni Seager's succinct formulation, 'Population control is a euphemism for control of the women.'[19] Finally, such warnings are illustrated by examples of risky reproductive technologies (such as the IUD debacle in India during the 1960s and the use of dangerous injectables) and coercive means (most notoriously, compulsory sterilizations and abortions), whereby women's health is sacrificed for the purpose of reducing numbers. Such measures violate basic human rights by compromising bodily integrity.

Pulling these different strands together, it follows that family planning programmes must not only be voluntary on the part of their individual users but also oriented towards women's individual reproductive health needs, rather than being designed primarily for wider socio-demographic (and a fortiori post-colonial) purposes. In formulating these objections, the Women's Movement focuses especially on situations where women's choices not to use (certain kinds of) birth control or to settle for small families are contrary to population stabilization goals, yet are judged valid expressions of their reproductive autonomy. Susan Himmelweit's historical note is instructive here. Initially, she observes, reproductive rights meant women's right *not* to reproduce through access to free, safe contraception and abortion. Later, attention shifted to women's right *to* reproduce, with a corresponding refocusing on sterilization and abortion abuse (and on rights to access infertility treatments).[20]

In order to address the questions posed at the beginning of this section and to respond to these feminist objections to population control policies, it is helpful to recall some of the theoretical disputes that inform human rights discourse, again starting with consequentialist ethics and its critics. From a utilitarian (Benthamite) standpoint, (self-evident) *natural* rights are meaningless fictions. Societies may nonetheless agree upon specific *positive* rights that are codified in and enforced by law. *Human* rights operate somewhere in between. They draw on moral intuitions that all human beings enjoy certain universal rights, qua humans, and are equal in this regard. Basic human rights, such as to life, liberty and security, are enshrined in international laws that may be backed up by international courts and included in national constitutions. They are not explicitly gendered, but their application or violation clearly has gendered implications.

Additional human rights that have proliferated more recently seem to be of a different order. They often entail socio-economic rights, or entitlements, and in this form they look more like ideals: ideals whose fulfilment is both contingent on competing models of economic structure and service delivery and harbours significant resource implications. Chris Brown thus observes that 'most economic and social "rights" are best seen as collectively agreed upon aspirations rather than as rights as the term has conventionally been used'.[21] In this sense, they function strategically by imbuing political demands with moral force. While advocates of women's reproductive rights recognize that broader structural problems of gender inequality require extensive systemic changes, the legalistic framework of reproductive rights appears useful for articulating women's grievances and demands.

It is sometimes argued, in a more materialist vein reminiscent of Marx, that if the criterion for *basic* human rights is that they are a precondition for exercising other rights, then a fundamental right to subsistence and the satisfaction of at least basic needs must be included. Yet this right is undermined by poverty and by degradations of the commons. If rights imply corresponding duties to rectify impediments, moreover, basic human rights must involve an obligation to ensure propitious material conditions, conditions that arguably include sustainable demographic and environmental outcomes, as well as adequate (reproductive) health services and equitable gender relations. In other words, satisfying rights in more than a formal, legal sense cannot be divorced from attention to adverse impacts from aggregated individual acts, that is, consequences.

Advocates of absolute moral rights understandably resist this reasoning. Logically, absolute rights 'must exclude any reference to the possibly disastrous consequences of fulfilling the right' inasmuch as this implies acknowledgement of exceptional circumstances for overriding it. Utilitarianism's critics draw attention to abhorrent policies that 'unrestricted aggregative reasoning might justify' under certain circumstances.[22] This slippery-slope argument is frequently levelled at purely consequentialist reasoning and it appears to fit with arguments for reproductive rights, inasmuch as population control is charged with 'aggregative reasoning' that may justify 'abhorrent' coercive acts like compulsory sterilization.

When expressed in this way, disagreement between consequentialists and moral individualists seems to result in an impasse between means and ends, or individual versus collective interests, except where they happen to coincide. This oppositional, either/or formula is illustrated by a recent intervention that asks whether it is 'morally permissible to interfere in human procreation through state regulations as to family size, or whether that impermissibly infringes on human rights'.[23] Yet this theoretical opposition is surely too stark to accommodate the situation in which such questions arise, where embodied individuals share socio-ecological spaces and have overlapping as well as competing interests. Between 'interference' and 'abhorrent' coercion, too, there lies a rich toolkit of policy options, as discussed in chapter 3.

Recognizing that freedoms or rights are practised or claimed within an intersubjective field suggests that rights might be differentiated and prioritized in relation to consequences, consequences that are not just an abstract outcome calculated by adding up utilities (qua subjective preferences, as aggregate 'happiness') but complex, messy outcomes that emerge within changing historical conditions which require ongoing assessments of relative, distributed benefits and burdens. Simply opposing women's reproductive rights to demographic and environmental outcomes is too simplistic from this perspective, especially given that women and their children comprise a majority – and an especially vulnerable one – of the planet's inhabitants, and that they are among the world's people who both suffer from 'the burden of human numbers' (Haraway) and share responsibility for and interests in ameliorating this burden. This fuzzier presentation may be less theoretically neat or morally satisfying than more dualistic formulations. Yet it can still accommodate a degree of inviolability for basic rights, while situating others within a shared political and ecological terrain that is sensitive to changing biophysical conditions, a position congruent with what was earlier identified as Mill's circumscribed consequentialism.

Amartya Sen's work is representative of this system-sensitive position. Sen rejects both purely consequentialist approaches that neglect basic rights and their counterparts that ignore consequences in favour of inviolable reproductive rights. He does not believe that resisting coercion should rely on disparaging environmental concerns about population growth or disavowing them as a racist plot. While acknowledging the existence of 'wildly exaggerated' claims, he does not dismiss concerns as unfounded. If the situation is not bad enough to justify coercive panic, he concludes, it does warrant decisive action to reduce fertility rates, using non-coercive means.[24] This balance seems to me politically sensible and morally defensible as an alternative to the more rigid liberty/rights versus coercion dichotomy that has framed population debates over recent decades.

In order to put this premise on a sounder theoretical footing and to address the IWM's criticisms more head-on, I propose distinguishing between three categories of reproductive rights claims, each having a distinctive level of inviolability vis-à-vis demographic consequences. They are: basic human rights (a universal right not to suffer violence and coercion that in this case refers especially to violations of women's bodies); socio-economic rights (in this case, a contingent right to reproductive health services that include but are broader than family planning); a moral right that is specific to the reproductive realm, as adopted by the UN in 1966. This grants all couples the right to decide when, whether, and how many children to procreate, and is arguably the most contingent and context-sensitive of the three categories.

Women's rights as basic human rights

Basic human rights to life, liberty and security are not gender specific. They include all people's right not to be sexually violated or subjected to gross bodily harm, and they therefore cover the more egregious abuses of bodies associated with coercive population control (it is worth remembering that the main victims of coerced sterilization during India's Emergency were men). The 1948 Universal

Declaration of Human Rights protects the integrity of all bodies, including their sexual and reproductive functions. It prohibits violations of the flesh such as rape, domestic violence, forced or under-age marriage and female genital mutilation (FGM). This logically includes a right not to have contraceptive devices inserted, or foetuses removed, without consent. Recognition of the woman-specific aspects of these rights and their enforcement nevertheless remains lamentably deficient.

What a woman-centred approach to these basic rights brings home is that moral agents are embodied and that the way bodies are treated is mired in systematic gender inequalities. This includes reproductive functions that are sexually specific, but also the way different basic rights are prioritized. The IWM is therefore justified in insisting upon a more woman-oriented understanding of basic human rights and in drawing attention to their widespread abuse, including in some population programmes. This is reflected in a phrase popularized during the 1990s: 'women's rights as human rights.' Although there is a danger of sexual essentialism if women are reduced to their sexual identity or reproductive function, the equation highlights gender bias within human rights discourse (as male-centric in its construction of the rights-bearing individual), as well as in its application (which tends to neglect rights violations that affect women specifically). In order to endow reproductive health services with some of the aura and universality of a basic right, some feminists additionally argue that their absence equates to discrimination against women since this precludes their exercising other basic rights. This becomes impossible to the extent that they are denied the means to control their own bodies and fertility.

In sum, these are rights of the first rank, rights that can never be legitimately violated on consequentialist grounds. Indeed, even from a utilitarian perspective, permitting their abuse would compromise individuals' security sufficiently to outweigh any aggregated happiness arising from it. It is consistent with these basic human rights, which protect bodily as well as moral integrity, that they must recognize women's right not to be forced to carry an unplanned or unwanted conception to term. To force a woman to lend her body to the gestation of another being against her will, by criminalizing abortion or endangering her health by obliging her to seek an unsafe illegal termination, is a violation of her basic rights. It effectively enslaves women to other people's morality and biology (a fate eluded by men). Just as no woman should be compelled to abort against her will, so no woman should be compelled to gestate a foetus and give birth either. Yet, in 2013, fewer than one-third of governments allowed abortion on request.[25] Northern Ireland is just one example where abortion is in virtually every case constitutionally illegal. Coerced child-bearing remains far more prevalent than coerced birth control.

Rights to reproductive health

A second category of reproductive rights concerns the right to access comprehensive reproductive health services. Rights in this category seem to fit best within the category of aspirational socio-economic rights, given that universal public health care is not just lacking due to incapacity in poor countries but is ideologically resisted in some wealthy ones too. Although reproductive health rights are commonly associated with women's rights, the capacious definition of reproductive and sexual health provided by the World Health Organization (WHO) is more inclusive. For example, it informs Principle 8 of the Cairo ICPD's Programme of Action (1994), which urges all states to satisfy a universal right to 'the highest standard of physical and mental health' possible, through gender equality and 'universal access to health care services'. Besides women, beneficiaries in specific areas include infants, children and, sometimes, men. It goes without saying that the health benefits incorporated (such as improving maternal health and infant survival rates) are important both intrinsically and as development goals. They have since been incorporated into the MDGs and SDGs, although the (environmental) public health benefits associated with population stabilization are not mentioned. But while mortality decline falls within the WHO's remit and family planning remains a component, fertility decline is noticeably absent as a rationale for improving reproductive health services. This partly reflects the success of the IWM in changing the basic paradigm from population outcomes to women's health entitlements.

The IWM is not monolithic but an umbrella of women's organizations. Some simply campaign for better health services for women. Aspirational rights serve their purpose by imbuing their demands with moral force. But others pursue a wider political agenda of reconstructing the entire framework in which fertility is problematized, such that reproduction and service provision would be reconstituted from women's perspective. They are among the most vociferous critics of population control. Yet, in the first case, it is not self-evident that the disavowal of demographic policy aims advances their campaign, and in the second a human rights approach seems at best limited in the pursuit of deeper transformational goals.

For the former groups, aspirational rights to access basic (reproductive) health services can arguably be strengthened by applying a version of the materialist argument mentioned earlier: that, in order to exercise basic rights (e.g. to life), individuals must have access to requisite levels of personal and environmental health. Thus, demographic concerns may not be irrelevant and their relationship to family planning services need not be simply instrumental. Provided that provisos about voluntary consent and basic rights are respected, I see no good reason why the family planning component should not be invoked strategically, to gain additional political and financial support from demographic narratives that recognize the social and environmental advantages (including for health outcomes) of a planet with smaller future generations in which every child is planned, wanted and nurtured within the constraints of planetary boundaries. From this perspective, it is unhelpful to cast population stabilization and its supporters as the enemy of women's reproductive rights, or to explicitly rule out the sort of demographic justifications for family planning programmes that can successfully mobilize resources behind services that benefit women. There is a caveat that women's health must always be paramount when providing contraception, with more research on birth control methods needed. But since fertility decline has no longer been ring-fenced because of its wider advantages, foreign aid and under-funded health budgets have been diverted elsewhere, as demographers predicted, thus further undermining efforts by less developed regions to complete transition or satisfy the 'unmet need' of more than 200 million women for family planning services.

In fact, the transnational position is less clear than the Cairo consensus suggests. True, the UN's summary of the 1994 ICPD proceedings emphasizes the new focus on 'meeting the needs of individuals within the framework of universally recognized human rights standards instead of merely meeting demographic goals'.[26] It thereby iterates the international paradigm that has been dominant since. Yet the 'merely' is important. Rather than simply opposing individual rights to demographic goals, the conference's Programme of Action had recognized their compatibility. Since

> the ultimate goal is the improvement of the quality of life of present and future generations, *the objective*

> *is to facilitate the demographic transition as soon as possible* in countries where there is an imbalance between demographic rates and social, economic and environmental goals, *while fully respecting human rights*. This process will *contribute to the stabilization of the world population*, and, together with changes in unsustainable patterns of production and consumption, to sustainable development and economic growth. (Italics added)[27]

Despite the terminological change, the Programme acknowledges that neo-Malthusian measures are both efficacious for improving quality of life and compatible with voluntary consent, provided appropriately non-coercive means are deployed. This is accompanied by calls for young people to be given responsibility 'to ensure that every child is a wanted child', but also by a conclusion that 'family planning and contraceptive supplies will need to expand very rapidly over the next several years':[28] the view the UN reiterates in 2017 and a plea that supports women's aspirations for comprehensive reproductive health services.

For the latter, more radical groups, it is germane to ask how well the human rights approach actually serves their ambition of advancing gender equality through fundamental social change. Its formal, legalistic framework is surely limited. Critical 'scrutiny of customary laws and practices of cultures which conflict with women's rights as human rights' is a crucial complement.[29] Yet this scrutiny must also include an assessment of human rights discourse itself since critics are aware that its emphasis on personal autonomy and choice may reproduce customary and practical gender bias. Corrêa echoes earlier feminist misgivings in noting that human rights discourse draws on western concepts predicated on a (masculinist) premise of possessive individualism, in which rights to self-determination are socially disembedded.[30] Yet social embeddedness again implies a broader realm of intersubjective life that is ineluctably located in, and enmeshed with, broader biophysical and socio-economic systems, as well as patriarchal structures. Human rights are therefore neither theoretically innocent in their gendered assumptions nor adequate on their own for achieving gender equality. This does not deny their usefulness, but it does underscore their limitations in transforming deeper inegalitarian cultures and sustaining environmental integrity, goals that might themselves benefit from fewer people and whose advancement requires continuous attention to collective outcomes. Recent developments highlight the importance of maintaining a critical attitude towards rights discourses and their ideological context. Since the highpoint of IWM attacks on population control during the mid-1990s, the global merging of political conceptions of individual rights with economic notions of subjective choice has continued apace. When the Global Network for Reproductive Rights concludes that the 'neoliberal restructuring of Third World economies' has had 'a devastating impact on the public provision of health care, particularly for women and children', it confirms feminist misgivings about relying on formal, individualist approaches.[31]

The foregoing discussion acknowledges the importance of the second category of reproductive rights as women's health rights. Two possible implications have, however, emerged. On the one hand, such rights have been ranked below basic human rights inasmuch as they are aspirational, socio-economic rights dependent on broader political, ideological and fiscal conditions. They have moral force but they remain relative and contingent, rather than absolute and universal, because their satisfaction is context dependent. They endow the provision of women's reproductive health services with moral force, justifiably emphasizing the intrinsic value of women's well-being. I have argued, nonetheless, that it is unnecessary and unhelpful to present these rights as essentially antithetical and hostile to population stabilization policies, beyond insisting that basic human rights are respected. On the other hand, if reproductive health rights are recognized as a material condition for exercising other more basic rights (to life, liberty and security), this inflates their importance but draws attention to their embeddedness within a wider biosocial fabric. Since collective, structural outcomes matter here, it is unhelpful to pit individual rights against consequentialist reasoning. A reproductive rights approach has, finally, been deemed inadequate for pursuing the wider aim of achieving gender equality, which requires a more extensive engagement with the numerous and profound ways in which women's basic rights are routinely violated.

Reproductive rights as procreative rights

A third set of reproductive rights concerns the post-1966 recognition of a right to choose family size. It is clearly restated in the Cairo Programme of Action (Principle 8): 'all couples and individuals have the basic right to decide freely and responsibly the number and spacing of their children and to have the information, education and means to do so.' Based on the UN's summary of this right's provenance, it seems clear that its original motivation was to satisfy parental desire for the means and knowledge to plan (and space) their children, without which choice is illusory. The underlying rationale was clearly not to facilitate large families since these are implicitly understood as a default outcome where planning fails and choice is absent.[32] Early versions present the right to use birth control as a condition of gender equality, not as a vehicle for attacking neo-Malthusian policies. Given that some 40 per cent of conceptions worldwide are estimated to be unplanned, and that there remains significant unsatisfied demand for high-quality family planning services, providing couples with the means to make genuine procreative choices would represent a massive contribution to satisfying all three categories of reproductive health rights.

The relative importance of rights and responsibilities remains vague here. Is there a right to choose irresponsibly, regardless of the consequences for others? The allusion to responsibilities suggests that this may not after all be an absolute, disembedded right that sanctifies what some would define as merely lifestyle preferences. This is Sarah Conly's contention in her book *One Child: Do We Have a Right to More?* (2016), which has recently reopened debates about this category of reproductive rights. Conly argues that a right to procreate does not entail a right to do so without restraint.[33] She invokes the kind of environmental concerns discussed in chapter 1 and draws from them a robust assertion that the best way to achieve sustainability is for governments to regulate procreation through a one-child policy. This, Conly reasons, would swiftly shrink population to a sustainable number, whereupon regulations could be modified.

What is interesting about Conly's argument is the way it reinterprets the nature of a procreative right in order to justify limiting couples to a single biological child. Inasmuch as there is a self-regarding (basic) right to procreate at all (and she is not entirely convinced there is), she configures it as a right to personal fulfilment from raising one's natural offspring. For this, a single child is deemed sufficient. Conly insists that there cannot be a right to more because nobody requires (has a 'fundamental interest' in) more than one child in order to live a minimally decent life. This analytical move allows her to avoid arguing for a temporary suspension or overriding of rights by asserting that no (moral) right to unlimited reproduction exists in the first place. After one child, governments may therefore legitimately specify the number of additional offspring permitted, depending on circumstances. Conly does recognize a more basic set of human rights (similar to those identified above) whose abuse is not permissible. But because family size is a lifestyle choice, it does not figure among them. Since she takes the unsustainability of current (population and consumption) growth rates to be incontestable, and sees little evidence of self-imposed limits, Conly maintains that it is confused and naive not to countenance regulatory action on the grounds that voluntary compliance can be relied upon or is inviolable.[34]

Conly's argument bears hallmarks of Mill's circumscribed consequentialism, but I think her one-child policy would falter when confronted with the kind of deliberation Mill requires before regulating other-regarding acts. In less developed rural economies without social security systems, larger families may be a rational economic, rather than merely a lifestyle, choice. The Chinese example, moreover, shows a single-child family norm is susceptible to adverse unintended but now well-documented consequences (selfish singletons, heavy family burdens on the young, a skewed gender ratio, rapid population ageing). Replacement-level two-child policy anyway seems more intuitively appealing and therefore more likely to win voluntary compliance and democratic assent. If it were accepted as a maximum, the number likely to produce fewer would probably suppress the TFR below replacement level, resulting in the sort of gradual population decline commended earlier. Regardless of precise numbers, though, it is Conly's support for a regulatory regime that is most significant. After a basic right to reproduce has been safeguarded, further procreation is classified as other-regarding and hence as amenable to legitimate interference, provided certain safeguards are accepted. Having dispensed with moral arguments against intervention, Conly focuses on the kind of basic rights-compatible measures that are available for anti-natalist purposes.

Elizabeth Cripps advances a somewhat similar argument but from a social justice perspective. She argues that failing to make hard moral choices to restrict population growth now may result in more tragic options later.[35] Alongside the (normatively easy) supply of reproductive health services, her hard choices mean considering mildly coercive 'incentive-changing' measures. The tragic choices that may ensue from failing to manage population growth now may entail more coercive instruments later. Like Conly, Cripps distinguishes between a fundamental interest in experiencing parenthood and a lifestyle preference for unlimited progeny. 'We need not assume an all-trumping, interest-based right in choosing family size which renders impermissible any collective action to influence procreative behaviour. However, a constraint has been introduced. Incentive-changing population policies can stay on the table, but only once the opportunity to parent at all has been secured.'[36] Once a basic right to parent a child has been recognized, Cripps allows a ratcheting up of incentives following first births. Her social justice concerns about the differential effects of such measures nevertheless add an important layer to considerations of just what kind of anti-natalist means are acceptable (see chapter 3).

Conclusion

This chapter has distinguished between three categories of reproductive rights: inviolable *basic rights* that offer universal safeguards against the violation of women's bodies; *reproductive health rights* that are unequivocally beneficial but aspirational and contingent on wider economic and ideological conditions; and *procreative rights* that are recognized by the UN but which environmental critics would limit to a single self-regarding act of parenting, with further procreation becoming an other-regarding act that may be regulated according to its ecological impact. This tripartite division is designed to put theoretical flesh on a mediated position (circumscribed consequentialism) that safeguards basic rights (and self-regarding acts), while recognizing other rights as dependent on circumstances (as embedded) and therefore as legitimately amenable to political interventions designed to secure the commons. It is nonetheless important to remember that these are moral rights that are regularly abused in practice. The argument rules out a strict moral or political opposition between rights or liberties, and outcomes or consequences, as well as a rigid libertarian dichotomy between individual and society/state. It provides legal safeguards against some measures associated with population control but not others. Having ruled out intransigent in-principle arguments against anti-natalist population policies, the remaining question is whether efficacious but permissible means are available for reducing fertility rates. This is the subject of the next chapter.

3

The Means of Population Governance

Arguments for and against pursuing demographic goals have now been considered, as have ethical objections to population control. A provisional conclusion has suggested that, provided basic human rights are protected, it is not in principle illegitimate for states to intervene in reproductive conduct. Action is only, however, justified if a convincing, evidence-based case is made for its current and future benefits, and following public discussion. The first proviso defers to liberal principles; the second satisfies democratic criteria and is necessary, too, for mobilizing public opinion and compliance. *Informed* debate is especially crucial when considering population matters, given their susceptibility to populism and social injustice. But supporters of inaction or pro-natalism are equally obliged to make a robust case for these options, rather than treating them as a default. There is a further, practical, proviso: there must exist effective but ethically permissible (i.e. basic rights-compliant) means for influencing fertility rates. These means are the topic of the current chapter, which focuses on the practical, political aspects of what might more appropriately be called population governance than control. It asks what 'control' and 'coercion' mean in the context of contemporary liberal-democratic governance and examines the mechanisms actually used by, or available to, twenty-first century states with demographic ambitions.

Because it is anti-natalist policies that are typically charged with using unethical means, these are again the main focus. In practice, many of the measures mentioned for modifying fertility behaviour can be and are used in both directions. Implementation of national population policies tends to mirror a state's overall style of governing and many of the countries currently facing the most challenging demographic conditions are not liberal democracies. Some are failed states; others are authoritarian, patriarchal or deeply divided. In response to enduring hostility to 'coercive population control', however, it is incumbent on advocates of stabilization strategies to establish that measures exist which meet standards of liberal-democratic government. This standard is derived in the following discussion not just from abstract liberal ideals but also from the way governing occurs in liberal states. It may thus serve as a political model for any state with demographic aims and provide an ethical framework for transnational organizations. This does not mean that hard choices do not persist, but this chapter identifies a practical framework for negotiating them.

Contemporary governance versus control

For modern liberal states grounded in the social contract tradition, complete non-coercion is a political non sequitur tantamount to anarchy. Preserving civil society, including defence of individual rights and liberties, requires a degree of coercion. This is considered legitimate, provided it rests on consent and operates within constitutional limits. Although the state's authority is underpinned by its monopoly of violence, contemporary governments use the state's repressive apparatus sparingly since voluntary compliance is more efficient. This is achieved primarily through modifying people's behaviour. The law punishes transgressors, but it also sends messages about (un)acceptable behavioural norms that are reinforced by public education and information. Public policy adds a fine-grained system of incentives and disincentives (mainly through benefits and taxes) that is modelled on, and supplemented by, market mechanisms (prices). Such measures are considered by liberals to be unremarkable means of governance. Together they comprise a matrix of messages, rewards and sanctions whose aim is to synchronize private choices and public interests with minimum friction.

The relationship between freedom and coercion, or private and public, which this entails is at odds with the dichotomy constructed by opponents of population stabilization. Rather than the top-down, centralized and bureaucratic model of government practised in the mid-twentieth century and associated with (population) control, current styles of governance deploy a range of sectors, agencies and mechanisms for purposes of behaviour modification. They work in ways that are often invisible as forms of power, yet they penetrate deeply into private lives. Vigilance against state repression remains crucial, especially to protect basic rights, but mainly the new governance works on individual preferences and choice architectures before they are acted upon. It by no means follows that these practices are beyond criticism, or that they are devoid of coercive aspects. But two points nonetheless follow.

First, that it is hypocritical to single out population stabilization policies for condemnation inasmuch as they abide by liberal standards that are acceptable in other policy fields. Second, that should governments be persuaded that a smaller population serves the public good, then effective measures compatible with their normative sensibilities are available.

In fact, despite widespread condemnation of population policies, the majority of governments do practise them. In 2013, 81 per cent reported direct provision of family planning services, often explicitly linked to demographic aims. Thus, 37 per cent of the world's governments had policies to reduce their population growth rate, including nearly half of less developed countries and 72 per cent in Africa, while 43 per cent aimed to reduce fertility rates. Inversely, 20 per cent were trying to raise their population growth rates and 27 per cent to increase their TFR.[1] Alongside family planning services, measures commonly deployed for achieving downward trends include integrating sexual and maternal health into primary health-care systems, promoting men's responsibility, raising the legal marriage age and improving women's education and employment.

It is helpful in this context to distinguish between supply-led and demand-led initiatives. The former, which figure most prominently in the 2013 list, are in principle less controversial. Building state capacities to supply comprehensive reproductive health services is a key development goal but one that is also recognized indirectly to suppress birth rates through disincentivizing large families. Providing choice among a 'basket' of contraceptive methods; information about wider issues connected to family planning and reproductive health; comprehensive medical support for female reproductive functions from puberty to menopause; well-resourced healthcare centres: these, in addition to legal, safe abortion, are supplies that would ideally be provided universally in order to satisfy reproductive rights. Cripps summarizes them as 'choice-providing policies', the most unambiguously ethical way to attenuate population growth.[2]

It is the demand side, however, that tends to present more intractable political and ethical dilemmas, inasmuch as a population resists supply-led inducements. Recall that rapid population growth persists during demographic transition for as long as mortality decline is not matched by fertility decline. Where this situation endures, it is usually because the prevailing culture rewards large families and espouses pro-natalist values. Some women may wish to limit their childbearing but are deterred by husbands, wider extended-family networks and social disapproval. Social stigma may attach to barrenness or voluntary sterility; artificial birth control methods may be condemned as sinful, unnatural or dangerous; small families may challenge men's perceptions of virility or the state's understanding of its interests. When it comes to managing fertility, supply, but especially demand, issues reflect deeper structures of gender inequality. Large families may appear economically rational for individual agrarian households, but they also express traditional patriarchal customs that tend to persist in developing/transitioning countries. This is why many demographers regard cultural diffusion (of modern attitudes to birth control), as well as economic development, as a condition of fertility decline.

The challenge in engendering demand for small families is not simply to persuade would-be parents to recalculate an ideal number of offspring. Beforehand, individuals who may believe their fertility lies in the hands of fate or others must be persuaded to think of themselves as responsible reproductive agents. They must exercise this agency by making decisions and acting upon them since every act of procreative sex not intended for conception must be protected. This may extend only to spacing births, which improves maternal and infant health outcomes, but if the aim is also to reduce family size, then behaviour must be re-normalized, so that fewer babies become the rational and/or virtuous option. In short, family *planning* is not just a euphemism for contraception; it requires a reconstruction of subjectivities and a construction of agency. This is implicit in calls to empower women. While this is emancipatory, once women are incorporated into the public sphere they become susceptible to policy and market mechanisms that affect their reproductive calculations. At this point, their decisions can be recalibrated through dis/incentivizing inducements and pressures. It is here, where subjective choices and individual decisions are apparently most free from state control or traditional authorities, that contemporary forms of governance are most effective in managing reproductive conduct. But is this coercive?

Liberal coercion and its limits

This section analyses the political meaning and legitimacy of coercion within liberal-democratic regimes. While measures like compulsory sterilization and abortion have been ruled out as unequivocally and impermissibly coercive, the discussion now moves on to incentives and disincentives as modes of demographic management where the line between freedom and coercion is less clear-cut. Moral judgements are less definitive here because political judgements are more context-dependent, as illustrated below. A salient issue is whether coercion is a question of *agency* (specifically, of state power overstepping certain boundaries) or of *means* (the methods whereby compliance is achieved). Isaiah Berlin's and Robert Nozick's theoretical accounts of coercion are helpful for explaining the distinction and illuminating its political implications when used for demographic purposes.

In 'Two Concepts of Liberty' (1958), Berlin engages closely with Mill's 1859 essay but defends negative liberty more specifically against political coercion. He argues, 'I am normally said to be free to the degree to which no man or body of men interferes with my activity. Political liberty in this sense is simply the area within which a man can act unobstructed by others.' If 'this area is contracted by other men beyond a certain minimum', then 'I can be described as being coerced.' Coercion is accordingly the term Berlin gives to political constraints that arise from deliberate and over-extended interference with individual freedom. The essential question for him is not what form interference takes, even if it is legitimized by democratic consent, but 'How much does the government interfere with me?'[3] Absent the gendered language, does this not encapsulate the opposition with which liberal critics frame their animosity to population control, as a coercive invasion of private reproductive space by the state? Yet Berlin was aware that his conceptual analysis was too parsimonious to accommodate the way power actually operates. He admits that, in actual situations, civil society requires constraints on negative liberties. He became aware, too, that 'deliberate' political acts ignore modes of interference that transgress frontiers of negative liberty yet remain invisible according to his definition of coercion: such as measures that operate through subtle forms of manipulation at the level of preference formation and desire.

Robert Nozick discusses such measures in his essay 'Coercion', which focuses on means rather than agency.[4] Coercion occurs when one agent prevents another from choosing to perform an act. Nozick identifies the key mechanism as conditional threats and offers ('throffers'). At issue is not enforcing obedience by preventing bodies from acting but eliciting compliance by altering wills. In policy terms, 'throffers' are essentially incentives and disincentives: they outline what the consequence will be (reward or sanction) of making certain choices, with the aim of guiding 'voluntary' decisions along particular pathways. Although Nozick defines them as coercive, they typically operate through 'free' markets and, even when governments deploy them, they are rarely judged illegitimate in the sense that they violate basic rights. Indeed, 'throffers' have become staple policy levers for liberal states and, if they are noticed at all, they are generally regarded as compatible with personal liberty and consent. In their more benign form, they coincide with what Cripps calls 'soft incentive-changing policies', for example positive financial incentives to stop at one or two children. But context is important.[5] In some forms and circumstances, incentives, especially disincentives, may cross the line of ethical permissibility. India's population control programme provides a good illustration.

During the latter part of the twentieth century, India's persistent population growth not only provoked notorious examples of rights abuse but also illustrated the hazards of tackling demand-side deficits when official anti-natalist aims are thwarted by a pro-natalist popular culture with low literacy rates. It became apparent that building clinics to supply contraceptives does not automatically create demand for their services. Strategies for generating demand were therefore devised, which relied on mass mobilization behind the family planning programme and on increasing incentives and disincentives to a degree that became tantamount to basic rights abuse.

To understand this charge, it is useful to look at

India's National Population Policy, published in 1976 during the Emergency. This enthuses about the capacity of monetary compensation to incentivize sterilization among the poor (mass vasectomy camps offering cash and other material rewards had been successfully pioneered in Kerala). The intention was to increase such incentives, not just for sterilization 'acceptors', but also for the 'recruiters' whose task was to deliver sterilization volunteers. The latter included medical professionals, labour in the organized sector and members of cooperative societies, local councils and the voluntary sector. This army of minor officials was to be motivated by tax incentives. Teachers, railway workers and village health workers were among local people given targets for recruiting candidates and incentives to pursue them aggressively. The 1976 Policy notes that, in some states, incentives had already penetrated deeply into work and welfare structures, with preferential housing and loans being given to men who were sterilized after fathering a small family and corresponding sanctions being imposed on those who refused. Central government workers were warned to expect their terms of service would be amended similarly.

It is difficult to identify precisely where the line between permissible and impermissible strategies was crossed, but opponents were clear that it had been.

Most obviously problematic was the shift to disincentives: penalties imposed on unsterilized fecund men and unsuccessful recruiters, who were threatened with loss of livelihoods or subsidies needed to meet basic needs. In a situation where the Emergency meant a suspension of civil rights, and powers were devolved to local actors operating against a background of caste, class and religious divisions, mass fear and insecurity prevailed. Incentives were also criticized on the grounds that mass poverty means poor, hungry people are made offers they may feel unable to refuse. In such circumstances, it is impossible to distinguish between voluntary and coerced consent, so that dis/incentives become coercive in a qualitatively different sense from the kind of 'throffers' made in liberal, market-based societies.

It is for such reasons that using targets, incentives and disincentives to pursue demographic goals has been condemned (as it was at the 1994 Cairo ICPD) as an unacceptable means of population control. Yet it is appreciated too (as it also was at Cairo) that in less precarious circumstances, and where the costs of non-compliance are sufficiently mild for non-consent to remain practical, such measures are widely deployed as effective and legitimate modes of governance. Congruent with the argument in chapter 2, it would thus seem that within certain parameters, judgements about acceptable population stabilization measures remain contextual since their impact varies according to (regional) political and socio-economic conditions.

(Neo)liberal governance and the means of reproductive behaviour modification

The rest of this chapter examines the policy mechanisms actually available to contemporary (neo) liberal states for modifying fertility conduct. The political question here is not whether the liberal state is ethically justified in interfering with 'private' matters but, rather, by what strategic mechanisms it routinely manipulates reproductive choices. The mechanisms described exemplify neoliberal governmentality in which, as Foucault explains, interventions are 'no less dense, frequent, active, and continuous' than in other political systems.[6] This model of governance is not recognized as 'control' in the sense equated with population control, because it generates 'voluntary' consent to policy objectives through behavioural change. Dis/incentives play a central role. Two principal strategies are distinguished in the account that follows: social engineering and biopolitics. Both fall under the broad heading of biopower as Foucault defines it, where population becomes 'the object of government manipulation' but is 'unaware of what is being done to it'.[7] In the current analysis, however, social engineering is identified as a distinctive economic mode of governance, for which '*homo economicus* is someone who is eminently governable'. My narrower category of biopolitical measures refers to strategic uses of education and public health campaigns, although in practice social engineering and biopower are usually combined. This is nicely illustrated by a recent report that focuses on their use in reconfiguring consumer and reproductive habits.

> Probably the most important levers to change behaviour are education, the creation of economic (and fiscal) incentives, together with legislation involving sanctions for non-compliance. . . . Financial incentives may provide additional reasons for changing behaviour. If society as a whole deems a behaviour unacceptable or antisocial, peer pressure can be an effective tool for change. Suggestion via the media is important in changing attitudes . . ..[8]

Social engineering strategies

Incentives and disincentives are most overtly used in social engineering approaches. Their provenance in the population field is instructive. When neo-Malthusian aims resurfaced in the mid-twentieth century, experts acknowledged that both the means to influence fertility rates and their ethical justification remained rudimentary. They called for a more contemporary policy framework. This effectively meant drawing on games and rational choice theories, which were in turn indebted to an older utilitarian psychology. Jeremy Bentham had written that 'pleasures, then, and the avoidance of pains, are the *ends* which the legislator has in view . . .. Pleasures and pains are the *instruments* he has to work with'.[9] Market forces (which use price signals to discipline decisions by making them more or less costly) suggested an efficient yet apparently apolitical means for managing fertility choices (demand). If co-opted or simulated by government, they could also be harnessed to replace more overt and controversial methods of population control.

This new behavioural approach can already be discerned in Hardin's list of viable options for rationing the commons. Rather than trying to suppress the self-interest responsible for its tragic degradation, Hardin proposed exploiting it to engineer choices. Instead of direct prohibitions, 'carefully biased options' could incentivize constraint. Markets play an important role in rationing use of the commons, by privatizing and commodifying scarce resources (although Hardin considered their distributive effects unjust). Taxes can play a similar role and are more amenable to policy aims and democratic consent. Although Hardin calls taxation coercive, he stressed that this was only because the candour of the word draws attention to the costs (in terms of painful counter-measures) of overpopulation and overconsumption, not because he equates it with state oppression. Indeed, he contends that if citizens appreciate why the commons is ruined, it is rational for them to consent to rationing through (progressive) taxation, as a fairer option than unadulterated marketization. He accordingly presents taxation as a good coercive device for instilling (consumer and reproductive) temperance, provided the means and their purpose are explained and agreed upon. Hardin was especially keen on applying this approach to the reproductive commons, where he dismissed assumptions that appealing to social conscience would suffice to instil responsible childbearing. Limiting tax relief to two children, or using it to reward women for delaying their first pregnancy, was deemed more effective.

Using the tax/benefits system to influence procreative decisions in this way was seized upon by environmentalists worried about ecological harm caused by the West's population explosion. The first issue of *The Ecologist* included an article that recommended a programme of positive incentives for sterilization, plus annual tax-free bonuses for women of childbearing age who declined to reproduce in a given year. In a later issue of the journal, the authors of the influential *Blueprint for Survival* (1972) suggested using tax incentives, education and advertising to encourage small families. They also called for research on 'subtle cultural controls' and for greater understanding of the ways socio-economic circumstances may be exploited to encourage below-replacement fertility. Similar arguments were incorporated into the *Plan of Action* produced at the UN's first World Population Conference (Bucharest, 1974), which identified welfare provisions like maternity benefits or family allowances as flexible strategies for influencing family size. If early formulations of these policy directions were somewhat crude, the behavioural logic they exploited would become more sophisticated during the 1980s, as market mechanisms were used more extensively as instruments of and models for public policy making. This is exemplified by the New Public Management, an approach that both exposes more areas of public life to market forces and brings market discipline to bear on public services. This method may resemble the 'throffers' that Nozick identifies as coercive, but incentives and disincentives mobilized to modify reproductive conduct do not cross Berlin's threshold of negative liberty; indeed, they are justified as ways to increase individual choice. Foucault's commentary on neo-liberalism in *The Birth of Biopolitics* is informative here. He presents it both as a generalization of market principles across all areas of life (thus distinguishing it from its liberal predecessor) and as an intellectual grid. As such, even non-monetary aspects of the social system are subjected to market logic, which becomes the principle of intelligibility for all social relationships and individual behaviour even when they are not directly economic.

Behaviour within this regime is effectively understood as simultaneously self-regarding (individual self-interested decision making is privileged) and other-regarding vis-à-vis economic outcomes (an increasing range of apparently exogenous social and environmental factors is brought within the orbit of economic governance, on the grounds that they indirectly contribute to economic growth). Fertility conduct, child-rearing practices, ageing, family policies, are among the 'private' phenomena caught in the neoliberal grid as important areas for management. Population and the environment are presented, here, as so much human and natural capital: human resources and ecological services that require continuous investment and refinement. As Wendy Brown writes, 'market principles frame every sphere and activity, from mothering to mating . . . from planning one's family to planning one's death.'[10] A UN report acknowledges this trend towards greater interest in demographic trends, with 'far more concern about fertility levels' becoming a feature of recent years. In particular, it finds 'more low-fertility countries expressing concern about and adopting policies to raise fertility and high-fertility countries doing the same to lower fertility'.[11] That concern is being met through engineering reproductive choices. The crucial debate needed here is not, I suggest, an ethical one about legitimacy or instrumentalism but a broader consequentialist one about the direction of these policies and their environmental impact.

In developed states, measures pioneered by anti-natalists during the 1960s and 1970s are now used for pro-natalist purposes. Baby bonuses, generous family allowances, parental leave schemes, tax incentives, housing benefits and flexible work schemes are the currency used to incentivize more births in the low-fertility, ageing societies of the developed world. Subsidized childcare, crèches, early schooling, and tolerance of births outside marriage and of unconventional relationships are explicitly commended by European policy makers as ways to remove disincentives to parenting, such as expensive housing, inflexible labour markets or rigid sex roles and gender identities. Fertility recovery in Northern Europe is accredited to measures designed to alleviate the opportunity costs of child rearing, especially those that enable women (and preferably men, too) to combine production with reproduction.[12] While the new pro-natalism is driven mainly by economic concerns, its policy instruments are justified by surveys showing that 'Europeans would like to have more children' (usually two, sometimes more) but 'are discouraged from doing so by the kinds of problems that limit their freedom of choice'.[13] The concept of 'unmet need' (desire/demand) is reoriented here towards pro-natalist purposes. Esping-Andersen and Billari identify 'a demographic reversal. This suggests that the "less family" trend was transitory rather than the harbinger of a new era.'[14] They expect it to become more widespread as family-friendly policies expand, especially among the middle class (they do not consider the environmental implications). Paradoxically, raising fertility levels requires expensive government incentives (like subsidized childcare) to counteract market disincentives that suppress them. For couples experiencing neoliberal austerity, relying on their persistence may be a risky choice.

Socially engineering choices through carefully calibrated incentives and disincentives is not of course limited to demographic matters. Advertising and other marketing strategies are widely used to reorient consumer choice and increase consumption. But government interventions in price structures, with the aim of raising the costs of polluting or incentivizing parsimonious use of scarce resources, are also common (justified partly by insisting that harmful externalities must be included in prices). Subsidizing renewable technologies like solar power is another example, although economists generally dislike subsidies, especially when used to satisfy demand among the poor for water, fuel and so on, which they charge with encouraging profligacy. Green taxes use similar calculations in order to reconfigure consumers' cost-benefit analyses. Thus the Royal Society's *People and the Planet* recommends measures like charging for rubbish collections, a tax on aggregates and installing smart electricity meters 'to enable consumer behaviour change'. 'By raising prices on less sustainable products,' it explains, 'taxes and charges can be effective in influencing consumer behaviour towards sustainability.' Inversely, incentives 'can come in the form of monetary grants and tax reductions and make sustainable choices less expensive', thereby letting 'the market play a role in changing purchasing patterns'.[15]

Because they are more visible as government interventions, and despite their greater accountability, green taxes are more likely to provoke resistance, both from vested interests (hence the fate of Australia's mining tax) and on grounds of social justice (since higher prices affect the poor disproportionately, although this is the case for all goods in capitalist economies). Governments may respond with compensation schemes. While welcome in social justice terms, however, they confuse the message (of sustainable use) and blunt the efficacy of disincentivizing strategies. As with other environmental measures, there is therefore need for carefully targeted, case-by-case assessments of policy interventions since disincentives need to be fair but just painful enough to deter extravagance. In general, commandeering market forces (for example, by allowing prices to rise in response to real or engineered resource shortages, as in carbon tax or trading schemes) is less politically risky unless policy makers can persuade the public of the benefits of a collective response to environmental degradation and of the higher longer-term costs of inaction.

Engineering reproductive choices is little different in terms of its mechanics from engineering consumer habits. This symmetry strikes some normative thinkers as morally repugnant. Yet inasmuch as policy makers deem it desirable to modify fertility rates, and they understand a principal mechanism of contemporary governance to be a process of behaviour modification achieved through reconfiguring costs and benefits, it is not inherently more coercive or unethical than other liberal-democratic measures used to manage the commons. Antipathy to population control often provokes hypocrisy here. When, for example, the United Kingdom's Royal Commission on Environmental Pollution (RCEP) reported on the environmental impact of population growth in the United Kingdom, it summarily dismissed population-stabilizing policies as unethical. Yet the Commission had no qualms about recommending extensive intervention in 'choices about behaviour and consumption' through 'sustained efforts using all available techniques, including regulation, incentives, education and persuasion'.[16]

While critics dislike the idea of couples basing procreative decisions on cost–benefit analysis, economists have realized that individuals cannot anyway be relied upon always to make rational decisions about their interests. Seeking more subtle methods of influencing choices, policy makers have turned to behavioural economics. A chapter of the United Kingdom's last comprehensive sustainable development strategy, *Securing the Future* (2005), was for example entitled 'Helping People Make Better Choices'. Here, the New Labour government proposed 'a new approach to influencing behaviours based on recent research on what determines current patterns'. The goal was 'measures to enable and encourage behaviour change' which address 'entrenched habits'.[17] This is the approach alluded to by the Royal Society when it recommends changing consumption patterns through 'intelligent ways to encourage, support and enable people to make better choices for themselves'. It was able to cite the Behavioural Insights Team, instituted by the Coalition government in 2010 and popularly known as the Nudge Unit.[18] Although it has itself been a victim of austerity cuts, the agency's work has been incorporated into governing practices based on the guiding premise of behavioural economics: that through an understanding of subconscious psychological cues and emotional associations that affect decision making, individuals can be nudged into compliance. This is congruent with neoliberal governmentality inasmuch as it works on 'interests, utilities, cognition, decisions, choices, actions, consumption, preferences, behaviors'.[19] Redolent of Foucauldian biopower, the Royal Society attributes its political appeal to the way 'behaviour is changed without individuals even noticing that this has happened.'[20] When applied to reproduction, such strategies may be unrecognizable as coercive population controls, but they are a method that is available for persuading individuals to make responsible choices while maintaining a sense of voluntary, if not necessarily welcome, consent.

I have suggested that behaviour modification achieved through dis/incentive schemes is the signature of current models of governing and is compatible with standards of liberal governance. It permits effective, legitimate interventions that facilitate demographic management. It does not follow, however, that this resolves difficult choices. If consent is voluntary, in the sense that governments do not compel family size, this does not mean choices are painless. For example, couples may refrain from additional children because they equate it with responsible green citizenship, or because they cannot afford more, but this does not necessarily mean they do not regret falling short of their ideal family size.

There are social justice considerations, too. In the previous chapter, human rights approaches were judged of limited value inasmuch as they are unable to address entrenched systems of gender inequality. Dis/incentive-driven models of governance similarly run up against entrenched systems of class inequality, in which costs of non-compliance tend to fall disproportionately on the poor and therefore look inequitable. Market forces are often praised as an alternative to coercive population control programmes in reducing birth rates. But as Demeny notes, while there is a 'tendency to idealize the process of development that historically led to fertility reduction as involving little or no cost of adjustment at the individual level', in practice it is economic hardship and deprivation that disincentivize large families and these are not costless for the families themselves.[21] Is the dis/incentivizing power of market discipline ultimately less painful, then, than if limits are imposed by democratically generated decisions supported by public services? An advantage of schemes that take political form is that policies can be deliberately designed to achieve desired (and accountable) outcomes. Where necessary, governments can redistribute income in ways that help compensate for unintended unfair effects. Perhaps the most obvious challenge here is to design a dis/incentive scheme that encourages fewer births but without increasing household (and especially child) poverty.

Incentives generally seem more acceptable than disincentives. This is partly, perhaps, why pronatalist policies appear more benign, inasmuch as they favour positive incentives and subsidies and are presumed to be congruent with a 'natural' desire to procreate. Anti-natalist policies that go against the grain are more often associated with negative, punitive measures based on threats of deprivation (such as China imposing a substantial charge for excessive children, which may be interpreted as a punitive deterrent or, alternatively, as a contribution to additional costs for public finances). The aim is not, after all, to make the poor poorer but to convince them to act differently (large families are already a major cause of household poverty). This is one reason why education and campaigning are vital supplements in gaining voluntary compliance. I have suggested that in developed, low-fertility countries, it may suffice simply to remove incentives to procreation and to publicize the benefits of allowing their populations to decline naturally. Yet, even here, a political decision against intervention is effectively a choice to allow markets to dictate demographic outcomes, inasmuch as low fertility is a response to the costs of child rearing. Education is important for wealthier couples, too, who may believe their ability to support more children justifies choosing a large family whereas, on the contrary, they make irresponsibly inequitable and unsustainable demands on shared resources.

Biopolitical strategies

Biopolitical strategies complement social engineering by re-normalizing reproductive habits. In the (narrower) sense used in this chapter, they work chiefly through education or publicity campaigns to reconfigure demand. Their aim is to modify subjectivities by disseminating desired norms (such as a certain family size) as standards of responsible citizenship. Specifically, their target is the public as defined by Foucault, as 'the population seen under the aspect of its opinions, ways of doing things, forms of behavior, customs, prejudices, and requirements', such that it can be captured through 'education, campaigns, and convictions'.[22] Although biopolitical mechanisms of discipline and normalization are diffused throughout the social fabric (for example, via the [social] media but also through laws and markets when they send messages about desirable conduct), the biopolitical measures specified here may be used more overtly by governments to achieve demographic (or other) outcomes. Thus, they support the kind of cultural diffusion demographers identify as key to fertility change. They are deployed in the public sphere as an explicit means of altering civic attitudes, rather than working indirectly through the calculus of individual preference sets.

Again, an initial deployment and justification of this approach can be found among post-war neo-Malthusians. Not all those concerned about a population explosion were enthusiastic about socially engineering the reproductive commons. Paul Ehrlich, for example, expressed optimism that a concerned public would voluntarily limit itself to replacement-level fertility, once informed of the reasons and serviced with the means for doing so. Such interventions are more obviously a legacy of Enlightenment approaches that emphasize education, on the assumption that reasonable, responsible decision making results from sound information and an enlightened interest in the common good. An enduring belief among many baby boomers (borne out by their own reproductive conduct) that abstemious procreation is the responsible choice suggests that such measures can be influential. Sex education in schools might, for example, include information about family planning but also educate children about the environmental advantages of small families. Publicity posters and media campaigns already emulate advertising techniques to advance broader health agendas (regarding diet, for example). They are not averse to using 'throffers', such as explaining ill health as a disincentive to high-risk behaviour. Saatchi and Saatchi's 'pregnant man' poster, used by the British government during the 1980s to induce men to sexual responsibility, is an iconic example, as are later television advertisements linking HIV/AIDS avoidance to safe sex. In India, publicity campaigns concerning maternal health, family planning and valuing the girl-child are prevalent on public transport and television. The efficacy of such instruments depends not just on their visibility, however, but also on the wider narratives woven around demographic trends and the socio-environmental commons. These largely depend on political decisions, which is why a new debate about the costs of persistent population growth is a critical aspect of sustainable development.

Conclusion

This chapter has shown that a range of ethically acceptable measures is available for modifying reproductive conduct. Among them, socially engineering choices and biopolitically reconstructing behavioural norms are indicative of contemporary models of government. These policy mechanisms, centring on incentive/disincentive schemes, manifest that particular mix of liberty and coercion that is typical of twenty-first-century (neo)liberal governance. Although their manipulative modus operandi is not immune to criticism, especially when conducted in clandestine ways that preclude democratic oversight and inasmuch as they disproportionately affect the poor, their application to reproductive behaviour conforms to overall standards of governing that liberals regard as legitimate.

In conclusion, it would appear that an assumed reliance on coercive *means* is not a good reason for refusing future population policies or the best place to focus normative debates about population stabilization in the twenty-first century. Instead – and given that most governments do, after all, turn out to pursue demographic policies – renewed debate about the purposes and merits of pursuing particular demographic *ends* seems more urgent. Chapter 1 summarized some of the relevant considerations, emphasizing in particular that pro-growth policies tend to be pursued for purposes of national economic growth and power, which are contrary to the interests of global social justice and planetary sustainability. From this perspective, I have suggested looking at such policies more critically, especially where they drive pro-natalism in developed countries but also where they are the default of patriarchal cultures confronting rates of rapid population growth that are contrary to their interests in development.

While it is important to revisit and understand the reasons (anti-natalist) population control has provoked such hostility, I have suggested that both the reasons and the term itself now seem largely anachronistic. This does not mean that critics' warnings have become irrelevant: they show how important critical vigilance remains in this politically and ethically treacherous field. But the benefits of population stabilization (and ultimately reduction) for the global commons, including for its poorest members and sentient non-human entities, are well documented and attainable by ethical means, if the political will can be generated. Getting the demographic dimension reincorporated into international environmental, including climate change, conferences is a small but vital step. Provoking new debates about the merits of population stabilization and decline, encouraging organizations at every level to embrace and explain this as a demographic goal and advertising the voluntary nature of today's rights-compliant population governance are even more important.

What has also nonetheless become clear from the foregoing analysis is that population matters and demographic trends are embedded in deeper structures of gender, race and class inequality. This is partly why policies in this area remain so controversial, but it also serves as a reminder that, on their own, population policies have limitations. Nonetheless, given worsening environmental indicators and continued growth in the global economy, it does not seem realistic to me to suggest putting the population issue on hold while these wider and more intractable problems are resolved. Limiting the human population may not be a panacea. But given that numbers are a multiplier of unsustainable behaviour, and that women especially benefit so much from the provision of family planning services that anti-natalist policies prioritize, it is surely time to return the issue to the political agenda. I have argued that political theorists, among others, have an important contribution to make here in developing an ethical framework commensurate with the governance models and biophysical conditions of the twenty-first century.

Notes

Introduction

1 United Nations (DESA), *World Population Prospects: The 2015 Revision, Key Findings and Advance Tables*, p. 8.
2 United Nations (DESA), *World Population Prospects: The 2017 Revision, Key Findings and Advance Tables*, p. 4. The *2017 Revision*'s medium-variant projection is used throughout unless otherwise stated.
3 M. Hardt and A. Negri, *Multitude: War and Democracy in the Age of Empire* (New York: Penguin Press, 2004), p. 166.

Chapter 1 Should Population be Controlled?

1 For more detailed discussion of these critical positions, see D. Coole, 'Too Many Bodies? The Return and Disavowal of the Population Question', *Environmental Politics* 22(2) (2013): 195–215.
2 UN, *2017 Revision*, p. 6.

3 UN, *2017 Revision*, p. 5.
4 All Party Parliamentary Group on Population, Development and Reproductive Health, *Return of the Population Growth Factor: Its Impact upon the Millennium Development Goals. Report Summary Update* (London, 2009), p. 2.
5 Sustainable Development Solutions Network, *An Action Agenda for Sustainable Development* (Report for the Secretary-General, UN), (June 2013), p. 11. https://unstats.un.org/unsd/broaderprogress/pdf/130613-SDSN-An-Action-Agenda-for-Sustaina ble-Development-FINAL.pdf
6 UN, *World Population Monitoring 2001: Population, Environment and Development*, pp. iii, 8. www.un.org/esa/population/publications/wpm/wpm2001.pdf
7 S. Caney, 'Cosmopolitanism and the Environment', in T. Gabrielson, C. Hall, J. M. Meyer and D. Schlosberg (eds), *The Oxford Handbook of Environmental Political Theory* (Oxford: Oxford University Press 2016), pp. 238–53, 240.
8 P. Cafaro and E. Crist (eds), *Life on the Brink: Environmentalists Confront Overpopulation* (Atlanta: University of Georgia Press, 2012), p. 264.
9 N. Keyfitz, 'Completing the Worldwide Demographic Transition: The Relevance of Past Experience', *Ambio* 21(1) (1992): 26–30, 27–8.
10 H. Marcuse, *An Essay on Liberation* (Boston: Beacon Press, 1969).
11 A. Dobson, 'Are there Limits to Limits?', in

T. Gabrielson et al. (eds), *The Oxford Handbook of Environmental Political Theory*, pp. 289–303, 301.

12 The Royal Society, *People and the Planet* (London: Royal Society, 2012), p. 83.

13 J. Rockström et al., 'Planetary Boundaries: Exploring the Safe Operating Space for Humanity', *Ecology and Society* 14(2), Art. 32 (2009), p. 2. www.ecologyandsociety.org/vol14/iss2/art32/

14 S. Wynes and K. Nicholas, 'The Climate Mitigation Gap: Education and Government Recommendations Miss the Most Effective Actions', *Environmental Research Letters* 12.074024 (2017). Open Access.

15 E. Crist, C. Mora and R. Engelman, 'The Interaction of Human Population, Food Production, and Biodiversity Protection', *Science* 356(6335) (April 2017): 260–4, 261.

16 World Commission on Environment and Development, *Our Common Future* (The Brundtland Report), (New York: United Nations, 1987), para. 4. 48.

17 For a rare exception, see D. Coleman and R. Rowthorn, 'Who's Afraid of Population Decline? A Critical Examination of Its Consequences', *Population and Development Review* 37 (Supplement, 2011): 217–48.

18 J. S. Mill, *Principles of Political Economy* (Harmondsworth: Pelican Classics, 1970), p. 115.

19 Mill, *Principles*, pp. 113, 115, 116.

20 Brundtland Report, para 3.2.61.

21 K. Williams, 'Space Per Person in the UK: A Review

of Densities, Trends, Experiences and Optimum Levels', *Land Use Policy* 265 (2009): 583–92.

22 J. N. O'Sullivan, 'The Burden of Durable Asset Acquisition in Growing Populations', *Economic Affairs* 32(1) (2012): 31–7.

23 J. Simon, *The Economics of Population Growth* (Princeton, NJ: Princeton University Press, 1977).

24 The White House Office of Policy Development, Policy Statement of the United States of America at the United Nations International Conference on Population, reprinted in *Population and Development Review* 10(3) (1984): 574–9, 575, 576, 579.

25 See, for example, Thomas Piketty's critique of Kuznets in *Capital in the Twenty-First Century* (Cambridge, MA and London: Harvard University Press, 2017), pp. 17–18.

26 D. Coole, 'Reconstructing the Elderly: A Critical Analysis of Pensions and Population Policies in an Era of Demographic Ageing', *Contemporary Political Theory* 11(1) (2012): 41–67.

27 See J. Repo, *The Biopolitics of Gender* (Oxford: Oxford University Press, 2015), ch. 5.

Chapter 2 The Ethics of Population Control: Reproductive Freedom and Human Rights

1 D. Haraway, *Staying with the Trouble: Making Kin in the Chthulucene* (Durham, NC: Duke University Press, 2016).

2 J. S. Mill, *On Liberty* (Harmondsworth: Penguin, 1974 [1859]), pp. 68, 69.

3 J. Waldron, 'Mill and the Value of Moral Distress', *Political Studies* 25(3) (1987): 410–23.
4 Mill, p. 141.
5 G. Hardin, 'The Tragedy of the Commons', *Science* 62(3859) (1968): 1243–8, 1244.
6 Hardin, 'The Tragedy of the Commons': 1245, 1248.
7 The White House, Mexico City Statement (1984), p. 578.
8 P. Demeny, 'Population Policy: The Role of National Governments', *Population and Development Review* 1(1) (1975): 147–61, 155.
9 P. Demeny, 'Population and the Invisible Hand', *Demography* 23(4) (1986) 473–87, at p. 476.
10 P. Demeny, Editorial, *Population and Development Review* 1(1) (1975): iii–iv.
11 Hardt and Negri, *Multitude*, p. 166.
12 See Repo, *The Biopolitics of Gender*, p. 108; K. Wilson, *Race, Racism and Development* (London: Zed Books, 2012).
13 B. Hartmann, *Reproductive Rights and Wrongs: The Global Politics of Population Control* (Boston, MA: South End Press, 2nd edn, 1995 [1987]), pp. xviii, 4, 6.
14 See P. Cafaro and W. Staples, 'The Environmental Argument for Reducing Immigration into the United States', *Environmental Ethics* 31 (2009): 5–30.
15 N. Rose, *The Politics of Life Itself* (Princeton, NJ: Princeton University Press, 2007), p. 66.
16 C. Garcia-Moreno and A. Claro, 'Challenges from the Women's International Health Movement:

Women's Rights versus Population Control', in G. Sen, A. Germain and L. C. Chen (eds), *Population Policies Reconsidered* (Cambridge, MA: Harvard University Press, 1994), pp. 47–61, 48.

17 M. I. Plata, 'Reproductive Rights as Human Rights: The Colombian Case', in R. Cook (ed.), *Human Rights of Women: National and International Perspectives* (Philadelphia: University of Pennsylvania Press, 1994), pp. 515–31, 515.

18 S. Corrêa in collaboration with R. Reichmann, *Population and Reproductive Rights: Feminist Perspectives from the South* (London: Zed Books, 1994), p. 5.

19 J. Seager, *Earth Follies: Coming to Feminist Terms with the Global Ecological Crisis* (New York: Routledge, 1993), p. 216.

20 S. Himmelweit, 'More Than "A Woman's Right to Choose"?' *Feminist Review* 29 (1988): 38–56.

21 C. Brown, 'Human Rights', in J. Baylis, S. Smith and P. Owens (eds), *The Globalization of World Politics*, 4th edn (Oxford: Oxford University Press, 2008), pp. 508–21, 516.

22 A. Gewirth, 'Are There Any Absolute Rights?', in J. Waldron (ed.), *Theories of Rights* (Oxford: Oxford University Press, 1984), pp. 91–109, 96–7; and T. M. Scanlon, 'Rights, Goals, and Fairness' in the same volume, pp. 137–52.

23 S. Conly, *One Child: Do We Have a Right to More?* (Oxford: Oxford University Press, 2016), p. 17.

24 A. Sen, 'Fertility and Coercion', *University of Chicago Law Review* 63(3) (1996): 1035–61, 1051.

25 UN, *World Population Policies 2013*, p. 68.
26 United Nations, 'Outcomes on Population'. www.un.org/en/development/devagenda/population.shtml/
27 UN, *Cairo Programme of Action* (1994), *A/CONF.171/13: Report of the ICPD*, para. 6.3.
28 UN *Cairo Programme of Action* (1994), paras 3.3, 3.5, 3.6. 3.7, 6.6, 7.13.
29 B. A. Ackerly and S. M. Okin, 'Feminist Social Criticism and the International Movement for Women's Rights as Human Rights', in I. Shapiro and C. Hacker-Cordón (eds), *Democracy's Edges* (Cambridge: Cambridge University Press, 1999), pp. 134–62, 136.
30 Corrêa, *Population and Reproductive Rights*, pp. 76, 77.
31 Quoted by Mike Davis, *Planet of Slums* (London: Verso, 2006), p. 147, from the Global Network for Reproductive Rights, *A Decade after Cairo: Women's Health in a Free Market Economy* (Corner House Briefing 30, 2004).
32 UN, DESA. 'Reproductive Rights'. http://www.un.org/en/development/desa/population/theme/rights/
33 Conly, *One Child,* p. 19.
34 Within this category of 'confused' thinkers, Conly includes Christine Overall's *Why Have Children?* (Cambridge, MA: MIT Press, 2012) and Bill McKibben's *Maybe One: A Case for Smaller Families* (New York: Plume, 1998).
35 E. Cripps, 'Climate Change, Population, and Justice: Hard Choices to Avoid Moral Consequences', *Global Justice: Theory Practice Rhetoric* 8(2) (2015): 1–22.

36 Cripps, 'Climate Change, Population, and Justice', p. 7.

Chapter 3 The Means of Population Governance

1 UN, *World Population Policies 2013* (New York: United Nations, 2014).
2 E. Cripps, 'Population and the Environment: The Impossible, the Impermissible, and the Imperative', in S. Gardiner and A. Thompson (eds), *The Oxford Handbook of Environmental Ethics* (Oxford: Oxford University Press, 2016). Downloaded from Oxford Handbooks online, 2015, pp. 1–14.
3 I. Berlin, 'Two Concepts of Liberty', in *Four Essays on Liberty* (Oxford: Oxford University Press, 1969), pp. 118–72, 122, 130.
4 R. Nozick, 'Coercion', in S. Morgenbesser, P. Suppes and M. White (eds), *Philosophy, Science, and Method: Essays in Honor of Ernest Nagel* (New York: St Martin's Press, 1969), pp. 440–72.
5 Cripps, 'Population and the Environment', pp. 4, 11.
6 M. Foucault, *The Birth of Biopolitics: Lectures at the Collège de France 1978–79* (Basingstoke and New York: Palgrave Macmillan, 2008), p. 145.
7 M. Foucault, *Security, Territory, Population: Lectures at the Collège de France 1977–78* (Basingstoke and New York: Palgrave Macmillan, 2007), p. 105.
8 Royal Society, *People and the Planet*, p. 89.
9 J. Bentham, Introduction to *Principles of Morals and Legislation* (1789), reprinted in M. Warnock (ed.), *Utilitarianism* (London: Fontana, 1962), p. 64.

10 W. Brown, *Undoing the Demos: Neoliberalism's Stealth Revolution* (New York: Zone Books, 2015), p. 67.
11 United Nations, *World Fertility Report 2013: Fertility at the Extremes* (New York: United Nations, 2014), p. 52.
12 R. Lesthaeghe, 'The Unfolding Story of the Second Demographic Transition', *Population and Development Review* 36(2) (2010): 211–51, 232.
13 European Commission, *Report of the High-Level Group on the Future of Social Policy in an Enlarged European Union* (2004). For additional EU sources, see Repo, *The Biopolitics of Gender*.
14 G. Esping-Andersen and F. C. Billari, 'Re-theorizing Family Demographics', *Population and Development Review* 41(1) (2015): 1–31, 2–3.
15 Royal Society, *People and the Planet*, p. 88.
16 RCEP, *Demographic Change and the Environment* (2011), paras. 6.33, 6.34.
17 UK Government (DEFRA), *Securing the Future: Delivering UK Sustainable Development Strategy* (2005), p. 6.
18 Royal Society, *People and the Planet*, p. 88. Quoted from the Cabinet Office.
19 J. McMahon, 'Behavioral Economics as Neoliberalism: Producing and Governing *Homo Economicus*', *Contemporary Political Theory* 14(2) (2015): 137–58, 147.
20 Royal Society, *People and the Planet*, p. 89.
21 Demeny 1975, 'Population Policy', p. 158.
22 Foucault, *Security, Territory, Population*, p. 75.